The MYSTERY FANcier

Volume 9, Number 6
November/December 1987

The MYSTERY FANcier

Volume 9, Number 6
November/December 1987

TABLE OF CONTENTS

MYSTERIOUSLY SPEAKING	Page 1
Cornell Woolrich: The Last Years (Conclusion) By Francis M. Nevins, Jr.	Page 5
Further Gems from the Literature By William F. Deeck	Page 31
Mystery Mosts By Jeff Banks	Page 34
VERDICTS Book Reviews	Page 35
THE DOCUMENTS IN THE CASE Letters	Page 49

The Mystery Fancier
(USPS: 428-590)
is edited and published by-monthly by
Guy M. Townsend
407 Jefferson Street
Madison, IN 47250

SUBSCRIPTION RATES (Effective with Volume Ten *TMF* will go to a quarterly publication schedule and the following rates will apply): Second-class mail, U.S. and Canada, $25.00 per year (6 issues); first-class mail, U.S. and Canada, $39.00; overseas surface mail, $25.00; overseas air mail, $35.00. Overseas subscribers please pay in international money order, check drawn on U.S. bank, or currency; no checks drawn on foreign banks, please. (Single copy price will go to $7.50.)

Single copy price: $3.00
Second-Class postage paid at Madison, Indiana
Copyright 1988 by Guy M. Townsend
All rights reserved for contributors
ISSN: 0146-3160

Mysteriously Speaking ...

In order to get this issue out hard on the heels of 9:5 so as to begin the new TMF more or less on schedule, I've had to go to press without most of the regular features. This issue will be in production by the time Marvin and Walter receive their copies of 9:5, so don't go looking for "It's About Crime" and "Reel Murders in this number. And the letters column, which generally consists of comments about the previous issue, is virtually non-existent this time around; indeed, it consists entirely of a letter from Jeff Banks which arrived to late to be included in 9:5.

I've had a few things on hand for a scandalously long time which I've been intending to mention in this space, but I just haven't been able to get around to them until now.

On hand for the longest time has been Walter and Jean Shine's *Special Confidential Report on Travis McGee*. This 42-page chapbook, an update of the Shines' 1979 "Confidential Report," is essential reading for fans of the late John D. MacDonald and his magnificent creation, Travis McGee. And to make it even better, the book is priced at a ridiculously low $3.00. Available from The Florida Center for the Book, 100 S. Andrews Avenue, Fort Lauderdale, FL 33001; make your check payable to The Florida Center for the Book.

Next in longevity (on my desk) is Sharita Rizzuto's new Sherlockian publication, *Baker Street Gazette*. I have the Premier Issue (Summer 1987) before me now. It is a hefty, eighty-page, saddle-stapled quarterly, filled with stuff to make Sherlockian hearts beat faster. Subscriptions are $10.00 a year; single issues are $3.00 each. Available from Baker Street Publications, P.O. Box 994, Metairie, LA 70004.

The last item is also Sherlockian. Bjarne Nielsen edits the Danish mystery fanzine *Pinkerton*, which I have received for years without being able to read a word of it. He also publishes, under the Antikvariat Pinkerton imprint, various books, including his own *Sherlock Holmes i Danmark* (1981). Fortunately for those of us who don't read Danish, Bjarne has just published—*in English*—an updated version of his 1981 work, under the title *Sherlock Holmes in Denmark: A Check-List of Danish Editions of the Canon and the Writings about the*

Writings in Denmark. It is a profusely illustrated, 66-page trade paperback, and Bjarne will airmail you a copy (in the U.S.) for 100 Danish Kroner. The address is Antikvariat Pinkerton, Nansensgade 66, 1366 Copenhagen, DENMARK.

I had a professor of ancient history at Tulane University, back when the sixties were bleeding into the seventies, who had himself graduated from Antioch College around the time of World War I (or The Great War, as it was, with perennial short-sightedness, then known). I took directed studies from him one summer, and I recall that in one of our conversations he remarked that his time at Antioch was a time of unrest similar to what we were then going through. He said that students at his school and elsewhere had been very concerned with what was happening in their world, and that the on-campus slogan on everyone's lips was "Whither Antioch?" The phrase has a striking sound to it--one can imagine Faulkner using it as the title of one of the novels he never got around to writing--and it has stuck with me all these years. I've never had occasion to mention it to anyone until today. But now, sitting here in my office, staring at the computer monitor and knowing that I've got to fill this and two more pages with editorial blather in order to get this issue printed and in the mail by week's end, I've finally found a use for it. For more that a few of you (better than half, in fact) this will the last TMF you will be seeing, so perhaps it would be fitting for me to use these pages to try to answer that burning question, "Whither (and Whence) *The Mystery Fancier?*"

Since it is impossible to know the future (show me a man who is absolutely certain about where he is going, and I'll show you a man who is, in all likelihood, lost), I'll dispense with predictions and just say that I hope that the new quarterly format pleases the faithful and acquires enough new supporters to make it possible to continue on beyond volume ten. At any rate, TMF will be around for at least another year.

What form TMF will take is, as always, up to you. Several correspondents have remarked in the past that they like the short articles that have become something of a trademark for TMF over the years, and I confess that I have a fondness for that form as well. But I like longer, more substantial articles too, and the change to the new format will enable me to run sizeable articles without crowding out the short ones. Therefore, I look upon the size-and-format change as an opportunity to add a new dimension to TMF without sacrificing whatever it is that has kept you people sending checks to me over the years. Of course, if you folks don't write 'em, I can't publish 'em, so I call upon the regulars to continue the good work, and I remind those of you whose participation in the past has been limited to sending me money (for which--don't get me wrong!--I am eternally grateful) that TMF was conceived as and has always striven to be a community effort.

Along those lines, let me restate TMF's policy with regard to contributions. Most periodicals, including mystery fanzines, gather contributions from many different sources. Some periodicals go after the best there is, wherever they have to go to get it; others publish any and everything they can lay their hands on, regardless of quality, so as to fill their pages. From the beginning—and with only a very few exceptions involving reprints—TMF has followed a closed policy with regard to contributions. That is, it has only published within its pages contributions from subscribers [or from individuals known to me to be regular readers even though they do not subscribe]. My purpose has not been to increase TMF's subscription roll, and if it had been it would have been singularly unsuccessful; there have been one or two people who have subscribed for a year and then let their subscriptions lapse just as soon as their articles appeared, but these folks certainly haven't made me any money. In fact, I'm inclined to think that the policy has actually alienated a few people who would have contributed to TMF and then subscribed had the policy not been in force. My purpose, then and now and for so long as I put out TMF, has been and is and will continue to be to provide a meeting place for members of the mystery community, a place where mystery fans can express their opinions and benefit from the responses those opinions engender.

I have wanted TMF to be a forum for mystery fans, and a forum requires two-way communication. It's not enough to rush in, toss your bombshell, and then be out of sight before all the debris has hit the ground. I welcome and relish bombshells, and from time to time I've pitched a few myself, but I can't overcome the feeling that, intellectually, there's something vaguely dishonest about expressing an opinion to an audience and then refusing to listen to the audience's response. The whole point of communication is to influence others, and there is something morally wrong with wanting to inflict your opinions on others without being willing to accept the consequences. It's rather like sending poisoned pen letters (or letter bombs). So what I have tried to do by establishing this closed policy is to facilitate communication between readers and writers, while at the same time keeping the writers relatively honest. While most of the TMF family is polite and genteel, there are enough of us unwashed heathens around to call bullshit by its common, every-day name, and the writer who gets pompous in TMF's pages does so at his own peril (as I can attest to from my own personal experience).

To wax philosophical for a moment—hell, this is the last shot I'll have at most of you, and I don't want to pass up this opportunity to bore you to death—it is an article of faith with me that if free discussion is allowed among men and women of good will, and is pursued by them in good faith, a close approximation of truth can and will be arrived at. On the other hand, if discussion is not free, or if it is not pursued in good faith, or if debating skill or flashy form is confused with substance, then truth will necessarily be the first casualty. All of which may seem a pretty highfalutin position for a mystery fanzine editor to take, but I believe that the position is not only proper and appropriate, but absolutely necessary. Even though we go through our every day lives without consciously holding the Yardstick of Truth up to every event, person, and utterance we encounter, we measure truth in our every action. Unfortunately, we all use flawed instruments to do our measuring, but even so, truth is supremely important to all of us. (Except, of course, to lawyers, for whom, at least when they are plying their trade, it is largely irrelevant.) No, I am not so deluded as to believe that TMF has any mission to play in Promoting Truth in the Universe; it's just an informal journal written for and read by a hundred or two very different people whose one common bond is an interest in and affection for a particular brand of fiction. But even TMF's total insignificance in the cosmic scheme of things is no excuse for not doing things right--and in TMF's case doing things right means providing an honest forum for the expression, and reception, of thoughts and feelings relating to mystery fiction.

This is the fifty-seventy issue of *The Mystery Fancier*, and I'm pleased to say that it hasn't changed very much since that first Preview Issue appeared late in 1976. Earlier that year I had announced my intention to establish a generalist mystery fanzine, and I offered to send a free copy of the Preview Issue to anyone who asked for it before a certain date. About 150 folks responded (of which fifty-six had subscribed before TMF 1:1 went to press). In my first "Mysteriously Speaking ..." I wrote:

> I had hoped to make this Preview Issue as representative as possible of what I want TMF to be like in the future--a balance of articles, reviews, and letters.... There is no letters section in this issue for the simple and obvious reason that, this being the first issue, there has as yet been nothing to comment on. That failing will, I hope, be speedily remedied, and I look forward in the next and all subsequent issues to a lively letter column with, perhaps, a healthy mixture of back-patting *and* back-stabbing. One of the few faults I can fine [sic] in *TAD* is the almost uniformly positive tone of its letter column. (That makes sense to me, though perhaps not to anyone else.) There will, I hope, be much to praise about *TMF*, but I'm certain there will be much to criticize as well, and the letter column will be open to all opinions, provided they are literately expressed and are not libelous.

That remains my hope for TMF's future, and I am especially hopeful that the new TMF will see the letter column return to robust health. It's been a bit anemic of late, so send along those cards and letters, folks. And money--be sure to fill out the enclosed subscription renewal form and send it and your check along to me as soon as possible, since the printer I've lined up to do the new TMF requires his payment up front.

Lastly, a fond farewell to those of you who are leaving us. We'll miss you.

Cornell Woolrich: The Last Years (Conclusion)

Francis M. Nevins, Jr.

When John F. Kennedy succeeded Eisenhower as president of the United States, many Americans (mostly in the younger generations) felt that a vibrant new era in their country's life was beginning. Coincidentally, the Kennedy years were something of a New Frontier time for Woolrich, too. He hadn't once left New York City since the 1931 trip to Europe with his mother, but now he made several lengthy excursions, using the Chase Manhattan Bank as his mailing address while he was out of town. In a 1961 letter to Bill Thailing, a Cleveland railroad worker who had been a staunch Woolrich collector and fan since discovering a tattered paperback copy of *The Black Angel* on board a World War II troopship, Woolrich mentions having spent seven recent months in Canada. There's good reason to believe he also stayed in the state of Washington, for in "The Maid Who Played the Races," a memoir he included in *The Blues of a Lifetime*, he describes how he was mistaken for a jockey by a cleaning woman in his Seattle hotel and jokingly offered a tip on a horse race which happened to pay off and led to his being besieged for tips by other hotel employees so incessantly that he wound up sneaking out of the building in embarrassment. Exactly what he did on his trips no one knows. Intermittently he would return to New York and put up at the Franconia, or the Gramercy Park Hotel at Lexington Avenue and 21st Street, or at some other temporary place.

On one of his visits back to New York he made an appointment with Edwin Singer and had the attorney prepare a new will. The document is dated March 6, 1961, and leaves his entire estate in trust to establish a Claire Woolrich Memorial Scholarship Fund at Columbia University, "to be used for the education of deserving college or graduate students who are interested in entering upon a career in writing." Chase Manhattan was named executor and trustee of the estate.

About once a month during the early Sixties, Singer and a Chase officer named Richard Keneven cabbed to wherever Woolrich was staying at the time and joined him for lunch. "He would order a beautiful lunch for all of us, with a bottle of wine," Singer said in our interview. "We ate our lunch and he drank his wine."

With Singer and Chase Manhattan handling his legal and financial business, and with anywhere from $9,000 to $15,000 a year still coming in from old stories and novels and sales to movies and television, Woolrich would seem to have had a perfect environment for writing as prolifically as in his prime. In fact he wrote almost nothing, and his hours were spent being gnawed by his private demons. "One day," Singer told me, "I got a call from the hotel [probably the Franconia] that I had to have him removed from there, because he was getting intoxicated, taking his clothes off and running through the halls in the nude. So I went to see Cornell, and he said: 'Why, they're damn liars. I'd never do such a thing.' I said: 'Cornell, if it be so, if you're going to be an obnoxious person, they're going to have a right to legally evict you.' He said: 'No way. We'll resist them.' So he did continue with the same conduct, and they did begin a proceeding to evict him. At that point he got very angry with me, and he went to one of my associates, and I was fired as his lawyer." But apparently not for long. "It wasn't long after that that I made an agreement with the hotel that he'd voluntarily move and I'd find another place for him."

Late in April of 1961 Woolrich went to the Astor Hotel for the Mystery Writers of America annual dinner, the first such event he'd attended in years. After the banquet several dozen of those who had attended went upstairs to someone's suite for drinks and shoptalk. As the evening wore on, the group thinned first to a dozen and then to about six. One of them was Donald A. Yates (1930–   ), a young professor of Latin American literature at Michigan State University and a fan and scholar of mystery fiction. Another of the half dozen was Woolrich. After several hours, Yates said in a 1986 interview, the six "decided we were going to go out on the town for what we didn't need at that point, and that was a drink someplace.... And the six of us headed out, and drove around town in a taxi, hit a couple of bars, ... and sat around until the sun came up." That was the start of one of the closest approximations to a friendship Woolrich ever experienced. "It was a long and glorious evening," Yates wrote in an unpublished memoir of Woolrich, "the first of many nights over the next seven years that I would spend doing the town with him, with this lonely writer who would never let you say goodbye until daylight was in the street. After a while he asked me to call him Con." The same nickname he'd preferred forty years before when he was palling around with people like Frank Van Craig.

"He seemed to enjoy my company," Yates said in 1986, "I think he liked being with an academic who somehow seconded his opinions, his views, on literature. I was enthusiastic about writers that he was: Fitzgerald, for example, or Faulkner, or Hemingway. He had all kinds of very shrewd and right ideas about these authors, about whom I guess he couldn't speak with anybody else. But with me felt he could, and I just made him feel good because I guess I was seconding his literary judgments on things."

He may have loved talking about Hemingway and Faulkner

and Fitzgerald, but he refused as if on principle to talk about himself. "He was made uncomfortable by references to his own work," Yates told me in 1987. "I honestly think that he thought it was so much garbage. Because he was never open to any query about [his own writing]. He said: 'Well, all of that doesn't make any sense. It doesn't make any difference. Why bother talking about that stuff?' And I said: 'Well, I happen to like your work.' He said: 'Well, that's your mistake. There's nothing I can do about that.'"

Whenever Yates came to New York, he'd call and make a date with Woolrich, "and we would set out, in the first of the evening's numerous taxicabs, to visit some of his favorite spots. I won't be able to forget the unconcealed pleasure he communicated over the phone whenever I called to say I was in town and had the night free. It was the pleasure of a child.... But what was hard always came later, when I would make a move to head home. Farewells were difficult, painful, and it always seemed that our friendship was washed up when I left him. I think I see now that he was afraid to be left alone." Yates was by no means the only person to be begged by Woolrich not to leave him.

Near the end of 1961 Woolrich did yet another of the bizarre deeds that punctuate his life. He filed a petition in the City Court of New York to change his name legally to William Irish. The petition was granted and the name change went into effect on Christmas Day.

Why on earth did he do such a thing? From what he told Lou Ellen Davis a few years later it seems to have been a way of striking back at his dead father. As we've seen, Woolrich had claimed in conversation with Davis that as a boy he and Claire had been gotten out of Mexico by Genaro just ahead of an imminent revolution, that neither he nor his mother had ever heard from Genaro again and assumed he'd been killed in the upheaval. "Years later," Davis told me in 1987, recounting what Woolrich had told her a quarter of a century earlier, "Cornell got a letter from someone who said: 'I am your half-sister by your father's second marriage.' And he was so angry that his father would do this, would be alive and not let him know he was alive and would remarry and would do this to his mother, that he went and legally changed his name from Cornell Woolrich to William Irish, ... because he didn't want Woolrich's last name any more." As usual when Woolrich talked about himself, he was lying, but with just enough garnish of fact so that the real truth is impossible to reach. He did change his name to William Irish, but he continued to sign his name Cornell Woolrich on letters and legal documents and to use the name on his fiction for the rest of his life. Was he afraid this alleged half-sister might claim some of his estate? Singer or any other lawyer could have told him that his will had already deprived any such relatives, if they existed, of all basis for a claim. Was he afraid the woman would look him up and try to enter his life? Any fool could have told him that changing his name to a pseudonym that had been known for decades to be his was hardly likely to stop her. In the end all we can say is what we have had to say time and time again. He did it and we don't know why. He was a man of smoke.

If there was one person responsible for trying to draw Woolrich out of his shell it was Hans Stefan Santesson, editor of both *The Saint Mystery Magazine* and *Fantastic Universe*, who took Woolrich along as often as possible to the gatherings of mystery or science-fiction writers at which, being involved in both fields at once, he was a welcome guest. Considering his reputation as a recluse, an astonishing number of his professional colleagues got to know him at one cocktail party or another during the Kennedy years. When I had lunch with him in New York in 1971, Santesson told me of how Woolrich would come to such gatherings, bringing his own bottle of cheap wine in a paper bag, and would stand alone in a corner the whole evening. If someone came up and told Woolrich how much he or she admired his work, Woolrich would growl: "You don't mean that," and find another corner.

Once in a rare while, out of such meetings a friendship of sorts was born. Robert L. Fish (1912-1981) had been a civil engineer in Latin America before turning to full-time writing and winning an MWA Edgar award for his first novel, *The Fugitive* (1962), and one suspects that the affinity between him and Woolrich was connected with his having worked in the same field as Genaro. With Michael Avallone (1924-   ), a prolific writer of private-eye novels, Gothics, movie and TV tie-in books, and anything else for which there was a market, the connection seems to have been that both men loved old movies. Avallone first met Woolrich in 1962, at one of the monthly MWA cocktail parties where he was serving as bartender. "I looked up from the bar," he told documentary film-maker Christian Bauer in 1984, "and this man was standing there. Drab suit, didn't know how to wear his tie, thin sparse hair, watery eyes, a little stubble—as if he hadn't shaved in three days, or the razor blade irritated him—peaked nose, a grim forbidding mouth, not talkative at all. And I said: 'Hi, I'm Mike Avallone. Who are you?' And he said: 'Cornell Woolrich.'... When I met Cornell Woolrich he was already dead.... I was talking to a dead man for six years...."

Certainly as a writer Woolrich was close to death. During 1961, although two of his Thirties pulpers were reprinted in *EQMM* and a condensation of the 1959 classic "The Number's Up" appeared in the girlie magazine *For Men Only*, not a single new word of his was published anywhere in the United States. Most of what he made that year, which totaled just under $16,000, came from TV and movie sales and royalties on his Forties novels. In 1962 four more of his oldies were recycled—one by Fred Dannay in *Ellery Queen's Anthology* (a series of semiannual paperback spinoffs from *EQMM*), two by Hans Santesson in *The Saint*, and a fourth by Leo Margulies in *Mike Shayne*—but a temporary decline in movie and TV money cut his income for the year to about $9,000. Three new Woolrich stories were published during 1962, only one of them at all memorable.

"Money Talks" (*Ellery Queen's Mystery Magazine*, January 1962), for which Fred Dannay had paid Woolrich $200 the previous year, is a pathetically weak imitation of Damon Runyon, set on the Jersey boardwalk like several of Woolrich's pulp classics. Al Bunker, a small-time hustler on parole, lifts the cash from a seaside concession booth and caches it inside a grape-drink dispenser before he's caught. At his parole revocation hearing, which ranks among the stupidest of Woolrich's many Stupid Trial sequences, the defense is taken over by Al's brother-in-law, a seedy medico, who uses some deviously applied itching powder to "prove" that Al couldn't possibly be guilty. Woolrich's original title for this yawner was "The Money Itch," and he may well have written it back in the Thirties. It has never been reprinted or collected, and the miracle is that it was published at all.

But Dannay was clearly determined to do everything in his power to get Woolrich functioning as a writer again. Just for the year 1962 he revived the annual short story contest that had been an *EQMM* staple from the mid-Forties through the mid-Fifties, and then at once awarded Woolrich the first prize for the story he'd brought from him for $250 back in 1958 and had been keeping in his pocket ever since. In January Dannay sent Woolrich a prize check for $1,150, and a few months later published the story, **"One Drop of Blood"** (*Ellery Queen's Mystery Magazine*, April 1962), which is in the "inverted" format pioneered early in the century by R. Austin Freeman and most familiar today from the *Columbo* TV series of the Seventies. A nameless young man unpremeditatedly hacks to pieces his inconveniently pregnant ex-lover with a Samurai sword, successfully (or so he thinks) covers up the crime, and then is arrested and brutally interrogated by a likewise nameless detective—who finally catches the murderer's one little slip and crucifies him with it. The story is so carefully written that one senses the meticulous Dannay standing over Woolrich's shoulder throughout, but manages to be genuinely *noir*, and very much like the 1938 Noir Cop tale "You Take Ballistics," in its use of the strategy of divided reaction: at one moment we want the clever cop to hang this smug, selfish and brutal young killer, and the next moment we want this trapped young man who killed in a frenzy of passion to outwit the sadistic detective and get away clean. Woolrich's notions of police procedure are as laughable as ever (unless you think forensic science can't detect huge gouts of blood on a wall underneath a fresh coat of paint), but the emotional charge of the story is far from a dud.

The third and last new Woolrich tale that year was not to Dannay's taste, but Santesson paid $90 for the periodical rights and ran it as the first of four Woolrich originals he purchased for *The Saint* before both the magazine and Woolrich died. "The Poker Player's Wife" (*The Saint Mystery Magazine*, October 1962) takes place in two rooms of a Manhattan hotel around 1910, a tipoff that this, too, was probably first intended as an episode of *Hotel Room*. Wiped out after a night-long game of stud, compulsive gambler Joe Talbot writes a rubber check to cover his losses. His pathetically loyal wife's desperation to recover the check before it lands her man in jail leads to misery and death, but the story ends on a surprisingly upbeat note.

The only new work by Woolrich to appear in 1963 was "Story To Be Whispered" (*The Saint Mystery Magazine*, May 1963), a simple and unsuspenseful piece for which Santesson paid $100. The tale is set in San Francisco on a Saturday night in the late 1920s and narrated, from the perspective of twenty years later, by a young man from the sticks who comes to the big city, sets out to pick up a woman on the street, makes a play for a young lady he meets, drinks Prohibition gin with her, is invited to her sleazy room—and inexplicably beats her to death at the point of intercourse. The text as published in *The Saint* leaves his motivation murky, but the version included two years later in Woolrich's collection *The Dark Side of Love* clears up the matter in a paragraph oozing with Woolrich's contempt for himself.

> ....But it wasn't as though I had killed another man. Or even (God forbid) as if I had killed a woman. Or yet (banish the thought) killed a little child. All I had killed was a queer.

The year that story first came out, a native Californian named Ron Goulart (1933-   ) was living in Manhattan and trying to launch a writing career. "I made it a point," he wrote in a recent memoir (*Twilight Zone*, November-December 1984), "to attend the monthly Mystery Writers of America cocktail parties, which I went to in order to meet girls, editors, or famous writers." On this particular autumn evening, he noticed across the room "a gaunt man, about sixty, sandy-haired, wearing a double-breasted tan suit and two-tone shoes. He looked like a ghost from the 1940s...." It was Woolrich. Goulart crossed the room to introduce himself. For the next few months, he says, he was part of that haunted man's circle of familiars.

> All the meetings I had with him took place in saloons, usually East Side bistros with the initials P.J. in their names. There was also a cocktail lounge in his hotel. When he didn't have anyplace else to go, he'd sit there and get quietly drunk. He told me one evening that the hotel staff looked after him very well and that when he was no longer able to walk, the bartender and the elevator man always saw to it that he got safely up to his room.

But after a while Woolrich got to be a pain. "His forlorn calls to join him at some saloon where he was drinking alone became annoying. I felt sorry for him and was appalled by the way he was slowly and stubbornly destroying himself, but I got bored. It was like somebody on a ledge who's threatening to jump—somebody who's been out there for, say, six or seven weeks." Goulart soon drifted out of touch, went back to California, and eventually became known as perhaps the funniest science-fiction writer in the business.

Woolrich continued to drink, brood and, very infrequently, publish something. For each new tale of his that came out, several old ones were revived—two apiece in *EQMM, Ellery Queen's Anthology, The Saint,* and *Mike Shayne* during 1963 alone. Thanks to more movie and TV money, and to a new paperback edition of *The Black Curtain* from the recently launched Collier Books, his income for the year shot back up to $14,000. Continued financial security didn't make him any happier. In December he turned sixty.

Woolrich attended MWA awards dinners only rarely and wasn't even a dues-paying member of the organization, but he was something of a living legend and did drop in on the group's monthly cocktail parties when he was in the mood to drink in company rather than alone. It was at such a gathering in or around 1964 that free-lance writer Lou Ellen Davis (1937-) got to meet him. Over the next few years they saw one another perhaps half a dozen times. "I thought he was very sweet and kind of lonely and I felt sorry for him," she said in our 1987 interview, "and he just thrived on people feeling sorry for him." He told her all sorts of false stories about his life and probably a few true ones as well. He even talked freely with her about his own writing, but what he said, or more precisely what she remembers him as having said, intermingled truth and lies with the same abandon one finds in his statements about himself. "He said that he wrote under William Irish because he wanted to save Cornell Woolrich for when he wrote something that would really be wonderful. But he didn't want to do mysteries, he wanted to do serious novels.... He said that he didn't respect the mysteries, that he wanted to do serious writing...." As if his suspense fiction both old and new weren't still being published under the Woolrich byline! But clearly at the start of his seventh decade his self-division and self-contempt were strong as ever.

He did seem interested in changing the nature of his creative life and perhaps that of his personal life as well. Lou Ellen Davis remembers another woman writer mentioning having had an affair with Woolrich around this time, and talks of threats against Woolrich by another man who was involved with the same woman. Publicist Anita Helen Brooks, who occasionally went drinking with Woolrich in Greenwich Village, says that she "didn't know him in the Biblical sense, though it wasn't from his want of trying." And he told Don Yates "that he had had bar girls that he would have relations with.... who would comfort him." Clearly Woolrich wanted others to think of him as heterosexual, but he was such a compulsive distortionist that, to paraphrase the last line of his 1945 story "The Man Upstairs," even when he's telling the truth no one can believe him.

In our 1987 interview Yates recounted another yarn Woolrich had spun for him. "He said that a woman he had met in a bar under certain circumstances produced a great sense of guilt in him. He sort of smiled in a bitter way when he told me this story.... He said he went to a bar, around Manhattan, some new place ... but he saw a girl at the bar, and she seemed attractive from a distance. He couldn't tell entirely what she looked like. So he ... came up beside her and asked if he could buy her a drink. She turned to him, and he was looking at the wife that he had married and walked out on. That was the gist of the story. And he was taking on himself the responsibility for that innocent, ... virginal, giving, kind, loving woman-- He was taking on the responsibility for putting her into a life of prostitution." In fact we know that Gloria Blackton hadn't ended up this way at all, that she had married again and that her second marriage had been, in her half-sister Marian Trimble's words, "a beautiful and happy one." On any subject under the sun, we trust Woolrich's unsupported word at our peril.

One evening in 1964 Woolrich somehow dropped in on a gathering of scientists and science-fiction writers calling themselves The Hydra Club. Hans Santesson was at the meeting but hadn't brought Woolrich with him. Also in attendance was an intense and rebellious young writer named Harlan Ellison (1934-   ) who was soon to become one of the science-fiction giants of his generation. "I wandered around," Ellison wrote in a 1975 memoir, "and finally found myself sitting on the sofa next to a weary-looking old man in an easy chair. Marvelous conversationalist. We talked for almost an hour, until I got up and went to the kitchen.... I described the old man and asked who he was." It was Santesson who told him that he'd been talking to Cornell Woolrich.

My mouth must have fallen open. I had been sitting next to one of the giants of mystery fiction, a man whose word I'd read and admired for twenty years, since I'd been a kid....
Cornell Woolrich!
Jeeeezus, if Hans had said I was sitting next to Ernest fucking Hemingway it couldn't have collapsed me more thoroughly.... Cornell goddam Woolrich! I damn near fainted.
I was flabbergasted. I'd sat and *talked* with Cornell Woolrich, one of my earliest writing heroes, and hadn't even known it. I wanted to find him in that crowded apartment and just be *near* him for a while longer.
They were bemused at my goshwow attitude, but they were also a little perplexed. Hans said: "I do not remember seeing him here. Where is he?"
And I led them back to the easy chair in the far rear corner of the room. And he was gone. And he was nowhere in the apartment. And no one else had talked to him. And I never saw him again....
To this day, I've felt there was something strange and pivotal in my meeting with Woolrich. He

could not possibly have known who I was, nor could he have much cared. But we talked writing, and I was the only one who saw or talked to him that night. I'm sure of that. Don't ask me how I know, I cannot give you a rational explanation; and I firmly do *not* believe in ghosts or astrology or UFO's or much else of the nonsense gobbledygook that people substitute for the ability to handle reality. But from the time I left him in that easy chair till the moment I want back to find him, I was right in front of the only exit from that apartment and *there was no way he could have gotten past me without my seeing him.*

Ellison's 1975 story "Tired Old Man" is a fictionalized version of the encounter, but we still have to wonder whether his nonfiction version is a true account or whether he reworked it until it had taken on the shape of a Woolrich annihilation story.

Woolrich continued to do well in the reprint markets during 1964, with one old pulper picked up by *EQMM*, two each by *Ellery Queen's Anthology* and *The Saint*, and a sixth by *Mike Shayne*, plus a new Collier Books paperback edition of *The Bride Wore Black*, with an enthusiastic introduction by Anthony Boucher, and a new edition of the 1946 collection *Nightmare* in Dell's Great Mystery Library paperback series. His income for the year, almost all of it from book royalties, amounted to just over $9,000. But the only new Woolrich material printed that year was a quartet of feeble efforts which Fred Dannay had bought from him between 1958 and 1963.

"Working Is for Fools" (*Ellery Queen's Mystery Magazine*, March 1964) is a pointless rehash, in radio-script form, of Woolrich's 1936 pulper "Dilemma of the Dead Lady," better known as "Wardrobe Trunk." Dannay, as we've seen, had permitted Woolrich to substitute this item for the 1930 "Soda Fountain Saga" when a legal dispute developed over ownership of the latter tale. The only point of interest about the radio script is that it's some evidence for the view that Woolrich himself had written the scripts for a few of the *Suspense* episodes based on his stories.

Even less interesting is the short-short of the late Fifties which Woolrich had called "The Jazz Record" and sold in January 1960 to the French magazine *Constellation*. Dannay paid $150 for U.S. magazine rights three and a half years later and ran the tale as "Steps ... Coming Near" (*Ellery Queen's Mystery Magazine*, April 1964). It's an occult vignette in which a father and his teen-age daughter hear death moans on the latest phonograph record of a pop singer who, it turns out, has just died. That's all there is to this quickie. If Woolrich's financial accounts didn't prove that he was the author, I wouldn't have believed it.

In the spring of 1963 Woolrich had sent Dannay a story he called "Four Sides to the Affair" along with a brief covering letter.

> F.---
> This is the jealousy-story I mentioned to you on the phone awhile back. It concludes the collection of love-stories I've been working on.
> It may not be for you, but at least I want to be able to say afterwards I showed it to you.
> C.

Dannay had liked it enough to offer $300, but as usual didn't like the author's title and came up with one of his own. "When Love Turns" (*Ellery Queen's Mystery Magazine*, June 1964) is nominally set in France--although there is no local detail and everyone in the story talks like a New Yorker--and, like so many of his late stories, it deals with the death of a person as the fruit of the death of love. The statuesquely beautiful Fabienne is married to the wise old philanderer Boniface but has fallen desperately in love with the younger and more passionate Gilles. When she learns that Gilles has taken a new and youthful mistress, she goes to his apartment to kill him while he's in bed with the new woman in his life--who turns out to be the new woman in Boniface's life too. *C'est Paris, c'est la vie, c'est l'amour.* Dannay apparently found a few holes in the story and helped Woolrich patch them up, for which he received the following note:

> Dear Fred---
> It's a pleasure to work with you.
> That's why you're known as the world's greatest living editor.
> Cornell

The last Woolrich tale for the year was "Murder After Death (*Ellery Queen's Mystery Magazine*, December 1964), for which Dannay had paid $250 in August 1962. It's another story of a loser at the game of love turning to crime for emotional revenge, but the protagonist this time is an uncharacteristically repulsive lout, and an idiot to boot. Georg Mohler loses the lovely and wealthy Delphine to law student Reed Holcomb. When Delphine dies a sudden but natural death, Mohler cooks up a supernally dumb plot to sneak into the funeral parlor, inject poison into her body and frame Holcomb for murder. Woolrich borrows his climax yet again from the ironic ending of Cain's *The Postman Always Rings Twice* but handles the details even more sloppily and implausibly than usual. However, the scene were Mohler hides in the funeral home and posthumously poisons his lover's corpse is a gem of poetic horror.

In 1964 the sight in Woolrich's right eye began to fail. Donald Yates and his then wife had spent much of the year in Argentina on a research project but saw Woolrich on a brief visit to New York. He "very nearly went to Argentina for an eye operation in January of 1965," Yates wrote in his memoir of the author. "He said he needed the operation. He claimed he had heard there were good eye specialists in Argentina. I told him he was more than welcome to be our guest, and we began to make plans. Things began to bog down when he found he needed to renew his passport. And when I couldn't free myself from business engagements long enough to take him around to the places he needed to go to make his plans—his eyesight was poor, and he wouldn't go out on the street alone—he slowly let the air out of the project. Later, in the States, he was operated on successfully for cataract."

Lou Ellen Davis visited him in the hospital and brought him a stuffed mouse with polka-dot ears to cheer him up, but it wasn't quite the gift he was looking for. "I remember he was trying to get the people who came to see him in the hospital to bring him alcohol," she told me. After his discharge he had a few people over to his hotel room for a party, the only known occasion on which he hosted anything. The stuffed mouse, Davis says, was sitting on a windowsill. "I brought him walnuts and a nutcracker for a present," she said, and got for her pains a cutting remark from Woolrich "about how he couldn't see to pick up the nuts."

At the end of April 1965 Woolrich felt spry enough to attend the MWA Awards Dinner at the Biltmore Hotel. Being Woolrich, he didn't bother to purchase a ticket in advance or to dress or even shave for the banquet. Gloria Amoury, then MWA's executive secretary, described in a 1981 letter to Don Yates how "an unshaven man dressed in a sports shirt and no tie showed up at the Biltmore just before we marched into the ballroom ... and said, 'I'm Cornell Woolrich. I have no reservation and no ticket but I was told you might be kind enough to let me buy one now and seat me.'" It was the only time in Amoury's near twenty-years' tenure with MWA that "*anyone* brought off the feat of turning up at our always-oversubscribed-in-advance bash in such a fashion, and getting the best seat available."

It was probably that same week when Woolrich had his first and only meeting with the critic who, earlier and with more enthusiasm than anyone else in the field, had recognized Woolrich's unique gifts and praised them again and again in his review columns. Anthony Boucher died before he could tell of the encounter but his widow, Phyllis White, was with him at the time and remembers it well.

> One evening in New York in 1965 we were in a restaurant with some MWA members after a private viewing of a film. As the group began to disperse, [*EQMM* managing editor] Clayton Rawson told us that before going home he was going to drop in on Cornell Woolrich, who was convalescing from surgery, and he suggested that we come along. Of course, Tony was thrilled at the prospect. We went to the hotel room where Woolrich was temporarily quartered. One eye had been operated on and he was to go back after an interval for an operation on the other. Hans Stefan Santesson was there trying to look after him. He was

supposed to go easy on drinking so he was sticking to wine. Santesson kept suggesting pleasantly but ineffectively that he slow down. The room had until recently been used for storage of furniture. It was in good enough condition except for lacerated wallpaper. Woolrich complained that the hotel staff was sneering and laughing at him behind his back. Rawson asked Woolrich whether he had anything lying around that would be suitable for reprint in *EQMM*. Woolrich rummaged around and turned up something. There was a bit of comic pantomime in which Rawson started to look at the story and then tried to hide it from rival editor Santesson peering over his shoulder. The only dramatic incident of the evening was missed by Rawson, who had to leave to catch his train. The door opened suddenly and a crowing man burst in with a girl and a bottle. The hotel had mistakenly sent him to that room and he was indignant on finding us there. Santesson attempted detente, ending with the grand climax: "... and this—is CORNELL WOOLRICH." The man stated that he was an American and not any kind of foreigner. The intruders withdrew, leaving Woolrich convinced that this was another part of the conspiracy against him. Eventually we left but it wasn't easy. Woolrich thought that people who went away, no matter how long they had stayed, were leaving because they didn't like him. Tony was delighted that he had finally met Woolrich, and at the same time thought that it wouldn't do his own nerves any good to see too much of him....

In fact they never met again. But apparently the cataract surgery was a success, for the handwriting in the 1937 desk diary Woolrich used as a business ledger becomes noticeably more clear and firm in the second half of 1965.

After recuperating from his operations Woolrich moved into the last hotel room of his life. The Sheraton-Russell is a quietly elegant apartment hotel at 45 Park Avenue, on the corner of 37th Street. Woolrich's final home was a comfortable if spartan suite on the second floor. Don Yates, who continued to visit him whenever he came to New York, described the suite in his 1987 interview with me. "As you face the hotel from across the street ... it would be on the extreme left corner. It consisted of a large sitting room in which there was a screen that he'd drawn across. A very small kind of a kitchen which was adjacent to the corridor outside. On the wall facing 37th Street was a sofa and a coffee table in front of it.... Looking out over south Park Avenue was a writing table and a lamp. There was a TV in the corner to the right of the writing table, and a few occasional chairs, [and] a closet which he seemed always to keep locked, next to the kitchenette. And then, occupying the space between the sitting room and the 37th

Street end of his apartment were, on the right, a small bathroom, and on the left, at the very corner, his bedroom. I never saw a book in his apartment. Never saw any kind of reading material, not a magazine, not a newspaper."

Soon after settling in he wrote Fred Dannay a note on hotel stationery, giving him the new address. "Sorry to move around so much. I don't deserve this final ignominy. Wish it were over." What he found ignominious about the place we can only guess. He did still write now and then, but left unfinished a great deal more than he completed. What did he do when the darkness fell? "From six o'clock on," said rooms manager Maria Garcia, who was interviewed by Munich-based filmmaker Christian Bauer for his Woolrich documentary, "every night, every evening," he would come down from the second floor and be, as she put it, "part of the lobby." Sitting in the same chair every evening, looking out the front door and window at the street lights, saying nothing, doing nothing. A few of the older waiters in the hotel dining room remember how he would come in and sit at a table in an alcove where almost no one could see him and quietly eat his dinner. He struck the waiters as a very shy man, but after he got used to a particular server he would be more friendly. After midnight, when the lobby closed down, he would return to his room, Don Yates told me in our interview, and "sit up late at night and watch late movies. And I know he would look for his old movies [that is, the ones based on his novels and stories] and see them over and over again." Mike Avallone had it right: Woolrich in the Sixties was a walking dead man.

For most of his career he had been represented either by himself or a variety of literary and media agents like H.N. Swanson. In 1964 he signed with the well-known Scott Meredith agency, and one of the first results of the agreement was the sale of a book to Simon & Schuster, which had published the three earliest Black novels before the falling out between Woolrich and Lee Wright. *The Ten Faces of Cornell Woolrich*, released in April of 1965, was not a novel but an assortment of well-above-average short stories, selected mainly from previous Woolrich collections, and with an appreciative if not too informative introduction by Fred Dannay to whom the book was dedicated. Among the seven tales resurrected from earlier volumes were at least three classics: 1936's "The Night Reveals," and "Debt of Honor" (Dannay's title for the 1938 "I.O.U.--One Life"), and the 1939 "Men Must Die"/Guillotine," here retitled "Steps Going Up." The three newly collected stories were the 1936 "Double Feature," retitled "The Most Exciting Show in Town"; 1940's "Finger of Doom," retitled "I Won't Take a Minute"; and the recent "One Drop of Blood," which Dannay didn't need to find a new title for since he'd published it in the first place. The back of the collection's dust jacket featured an excellent if idealized sketch of Woolrich by artist John Gaughan. Five years had passed since the last new Woolrich book of any sort and seven since the last hardcover, but critical reaction to *The Ten Faces* was at best restrained, and even Boucher gagged at the overfamiliarity of most of the selections. "Much though I admire the work of Cornell Woolrich/William Irish, I can see little excuse for [this volume].... The stories, to be sure, range from good to excellent, but this can hardly claim to be a new $3.95 book." The collection sold poorly and has never been reprinted.

A few months later came the year's second volume of Woolrich short stories and the last new title under any of his bylines to appear in his lifetime. *The Dark Side of Love*, subtitled "Tales of Love and Death," was the "collection of love-stories" Woolrich had mentioned to Fred Dannay in the spring of 1963. It was purchased for a laughable $600 advance in October 1964 by Walker & Co., a new and then marginal publishing house specializing in cheaply made U.S. editions of English detective fiction. Most of its eight stories were unsold to magazines and probably unsalable. To make things worse, the book's copyright page proclaims that it was printed from type set in Austria, which was a blatant confession that the publisher had violated the domestic manufacture requirements of the Copyright Act, with the result that all new matter in the collection risked being thrown into the public domain. In his brief review for the *Times*, Boucher remarked that the book "stresses [Woolrich's] weaknesses rather than his virtues." But it also gives us a concentrated dose of how the world looked to him as he approached death.

Fittingly enough in view of its theme, the collection is dedicated to no one and opens with a bleak quotation from poet W.H. Auden: "The more they love/The more they feel alone." The first story in the book is "Je t'Aime," which Dannay had run in *EQMM* the year before as "When Love Turns." Next comes "The Clean Fight," the last Woolrich story with police protagonists and one of the strongest. As in his Noir Cop classics, the officers are portrayed as gods (that is, malign thugs) with badges and licenses to kill. The setting is a pair of hotel rooms—could this be another excised chapter from Woolrich's 1958 episodic novel?—and we watch a team of cops carrying out a plan to murder in cold blood a terrified wretch who had been remotely responsible for the death of the beloved squad commander's only son. The religious language and overtones hint that God the Father and his archangels are avenging themselves on Judas for the betrayal of Jesus. By all normal standards the story is ridiculous—in three years none of the police assassins can figure a way to knock off their victim!—but Woolrich's intense evocations stifle critical thought.

The third tale in the collection, "The Idol with the Clay Bottom," dates back at least to 1944. In a letter of that year to anthologist Frank Owen, who turned it down for publication, Woolrich had said: "They don't come any more Rabelaisian than this one." Nor screwier either. Marie, an ex-prostitute determined to start over, falls in love with Don, who as a boy was physically abused by his sadistic stepmother. They plan to marry but Marie is terrified that she'll lose him if she admits she used to be a whore. Finally, just when she's almost worked up the nerve to tell him, a tavern barmaid accidentally whacks

Don's rear end with a tray. His face suddenly suffused with ecstacy, he screams at the maid to hit him again. Marie disgustedly walks out.

> He got up on one knee and called out to her. "Marie! Wait! Don't run out on me! Don't leave me!"
> "Geddaway from me!" she shrilled back rabidly. "You're queer for paddy whacks!" And again she ran, ran until he was out of sight and out of her life.

She returns to prostitution and one of her steady customers seems to be falling in love with her as the story ends. All we can say for sure about this wretched waste of ink is that at the time he wrote it Woolrich's own "queer" side must have plunged him into the depths of self-revulsion.

The next three stories had all appeared in print before in one form or another: "The Poker Player's Wife" and "Story To Be Whispered" in *The Saint* (although the ending of the latter tale is much clearer in the book version), and "Somebody Else's Life" in the 1959 collection *Beyond the Night*, as the TV script "Somebody's Clothes--Somebody's Life." Recasting the teleplay into prose didn't improve it.

These were followed by "I'm Ashamed," another previously unpublished tale of sexual-psychological horror, in which high-schooler Bruce Neil goes downtown with his buddy Warren for some Saturday night fun and the two boys wind up losing their virginity in a brothel. The next morning Bruce discovers that his whore's last customer before him had been his father, and in a fit of shame he hangs himself. This quiet slice of hell is evoked in vivid imagery ("The street-lamps on their tall hooked posts spit violet-white needles of light drowsily upon the roadway") of a sort rarely encountered in Woolrich's final tales. The perverse storyline and the protagonist trapped by a sense of sin can perhaps be read as correlatives for the special agonies of the homosexual whose religious roots are Catholic.

The collection closes with "Too Nice a Day to Die," a faultless gem of *noir*, its facets perfectly reflecting a world in which chance is god and beams fall. Desperately lonely Laurel Hammond turns on the gas in her New York apartment one morning, ready to end her life. The phone rings, and from force of habit she opens the windows and picks up the receiver. It's a wrong number, someone wanting Schultz's Delicatessen. The absurdity gives her the will to live a single day longer. She goes out, walks around the city, and thanks to the long arm of chance or fate meets a man in Rockefeller Plaza who seems to be as right for her as she seems to be for him. Then comes the third beam: as they're on the way back to her place for dinner, she is run down while crossing the road and dies. The world according to Woolrich has rarely been rendered in such fitting form.

While *The Dark Side of Love* was at the printers, Scott Meredith agents sold "The Idol with the Clay Bottom" to the men's magazine *Knight* and both "One Drop of Blood" and "Too Nice a Day to Die" to the short-lived new suspense-horror periodical *Bizarre*. *EQMM, Ellery Queen's Anthology, The Saint* and *Mike Shayne* each reprinted a Woolrich story during 1965, and Collier Books added the 1942 *Black Alibi* to its paperback series. Thanks to reprint sales and continuing media interest in the *noir* classics of Woolrich's prime, he never had to worry about where the next drink was coming from. His total income for the year topped the $18,000 mark despite the fact that he was writing next to nothing.

Every now and then he would make a feeble effort to break out of the box in which he'd locked himself, but each time he'd abort the plan in its final stages. Don Yates invited him to East Lansing, Michigan, for the 1966 Memorial Day weekend. In a letter dated April 30 and handwritten on Sheraton-Russell stationery, Woolrich more or less accepted.

>Donny-Boy---
>Thanks.
>I'll try to make it for the Decoration Day weekend, say like June One.
>Should I give up my pad here, and then just keep going after my stop-over at Lansing?
>Give me some advice. I'm not secure. Should I take a chance?
>I'm not happy here. I'll have to get a new passport if I do shove off though.
>I want to come by Trailways bus. Give me the shove I need. Rig up a schedule of some kind (of theirs) and send it to me. Exact times and stop-overs and changes, etc. Funny how helpless you can get. Like a kid almost.
>Con

Few readers will be surprised to learn that he never showed up. "This time," Yates told me, "the plans foundered because the Trailways line didn't serve Lansing. That was his explanation."

Later in 1966 he pulled the same stunt again. When Yates wrote asking permission to use his 1939 classic "Men Must Die"/"Guillotine" in an anthology of mystery fiction in Spanish translation, Woolrich readily agreed, but in return, he said in his reply letter, "do me a favor. Write back and give me the name of the best hotel in Lansing, so I'll know where to make my reservation when I'm ready to come out. I imagine around Thanksgiving would be a nice time. It's not too cold out there then, is it?" History repeated itself: he never came. Late in November he sent Yates a Christmas card with a quintessential Woolrich message.

>Hello, Pal.
>Sometimes I miss you. Sometimes I don't.
>Cornell

The briefest excursion out of New York seemed to terrify him as much as a trip halfway across the country. Over and over again Fred Dannay would invite Woolrich to spend a Sunday afternoon with him and his wife at Larchmont, which is forty minutes by train from Grand Central Station. Woolrich might answer with a Yes or a No or a Maybe, but he never came once.

Miraculously, he still managed to write a little and, thanks to Dannay and Santesson, to sell what he wrote. There were no new paperback editions of any Woolrich novel during 1966, but EQMM and *Mike Shayne* reprinted one Thirties pulper each and *Ellery Queen's Anthology* and *The Saint* ran two each. Thanks again mainly to overseas and media money, he made more than $12,500 that year despite having only two new stories published in the entire twelve months.

"It Only Takes a Minute to Die" (*Ellery Queen's Mystery Magazine*, July 1966) is a perfect Woolrich title, much better indeed than the story that goes with it, for which Dannay had paid $300 in mid-1965. Judged purely by its plot it's a routine exercise in the inverted form of "One Drop of Blood," with X killing Y in the first part of the tale and getting tripped up in the second by The One Little Detail He Overlooked. (That detail, a telephone book, was Dannay's idea, not Woolrich's. The correspondence between editor and author shows that Dannay found a gaggle of plot flaws in the manuscript as originally submitted, and suggested ways to eliminate them. Woolrich rewrote the end of the story in his own handwriting on eight sheets of Sheraton-Russell stationery, and with minor stylistic changes by Dannay, the published version follows Woolrich's revisions.) But thematically the story fits within the *noir* universe from the first page with its echo of Poe's "The Cask of Amontillado."

> Why he wanted to kill him need not be brought within the compass of this story.... All that need be said is that he wanted to kill him, he did kill him, and he botched it--and now let the story begin.

The murderer's name is Killare, the victim is called Dade, and the events of the crime are infused with religious motifs and a sort of ritualistic determinism, almost as if the two were celebrating Mass together, or making love. (The sex-death connection is exceptionally strong in the scene where Killare makes Dade undress and lie down in bed and then slowly strangles him with a pillow.) It's unfortunate that so much *noir* grotesquerie is thrown away on a perfectly ordinary plot.

"Mannequin" (*The Saint Magazine*, October 1966), which Santesson bought for $175, is a much longer and more powerful story, by far the finest of the four Woolrich originals published in *The Saint*. Its first half is a brilliant set-piece of suspense as Leone, a low-ranking model for a Paris fashion designer, is shadowed day and night for no discernible reason by a barely glimpsed menace. Only after several thousand words of pulsating terror-in-the-everyday does she learn that her lover has escaped from prison and that her shadow is a Javert figure who expects the fugitive to take refuge with her. The ending is as bitter and tragic as one expects in Woolrich, and the spirit is so close to that of the original French *films noir* of the late Thirties that one half-suspects the story was written at that time and kept in Woolrich's files until almost three decades later.

On a visit to New York in the spring of 1967, Don Yates "had a glimpse into one of the dark pits" that made up the Woolrich world. "It was a long, confusing night," he says in his memoir, but what he remembers about it most vividly is Woolrich's claim that he was "being followed, persecuted" by another resident on the second floor of the Sheraton-Russell.

> This man, whom everybody else trusted, was after Con Woolrich for something that Con didn't find out the nature of. When [Woolrich] left his room, he was sure that the man had come into the room and searched it. What he was searching for, he never knew. He never caught him in the room but lived in mortal fear of this man discovering something.
>
> He said the man had women in his own room, which was apparently some kind of condemnation of the fellow. He said that everybody else thought that he was a fine chap, but gradually, by talking to the administration, to the bellboys, to the staff, he managed to work up some opposition to the fellow and claimed that he was evicted from his room. He said he saw him later, in a restaurant, and the man acted very friendly then to him.
>
> The way he told the story, it seemed to me as real as anything else in his life. Of course, it's the kind of nightmarish concoction that he would devise for so many of his stories. It may have been that he worked with the theme too long, and somehow it passed ... into his own existence. It made no sense. He said that he knew the man was elusive, and he could never pin him down and find out what he was doing. But he knew something was after him for a long time that terrified him.

During that same spring Woolrich probably wrote and certainly sold the last suspense story of his life, and by a curious coincidence it deals with a nameless and lonely man on the second floor of a New York Hotel room who is being hounded for reasons unknown by Them. Could Woolrich have been playing a game with Yates, transforming that story into a sort of dramatic monologue? Yates didn't think so. "I don't know if that man existed or not," he told me in our 1987 interview. "But Cornell felt helpless to defuse what this man was doing. As if he had some supernatural power and could come and go and disappear and abuse the sanctity of his hotel room. He was angry when he thought about that man having come into his room and searched it while he was gone. He was absolutely physically showing the signs of anger. So it seemed to be real to me, in his own mind. Whether it was real or not, nobody knows."

If 1967 was a year of paranoid nightmare for Woolrich the man, it was a time of revival for Woolrich the writer. Not only did Fred Dannay reprint three more of his pulpers (one in *EQMM*, two in *Ellery Queen's Anthology*) and Hans Santesson run another pair in *The Saint*, but three separate book publishers reissued a trio of classic Woolrich novels. W.W. Norton offered a hardcover edition of *Phantom Lady*, Paperback Library a softcover of *Night Has a Thousand Eyes*, and Ace Books a paperback of *The Bride Wore Black*, the first of four titles from the so-called Black Series which the company would put out over a two-year period. That multi-book deal was made by a Scott Meredith agent assigned in June 1967 to the Woolrich account, an obscure young Jewish intellectual who on the surface had nothing in common with his client but in fact was to develop a deep affinity with the man of darkness.

Barry N. Malzberg (1939-   ) had a literary-academic background and a strong ambition to have short stories published in highbrow quarterlies like *The Hudson Review*. All he collected from those journals was rejection slips. Frustrated and hungry, he had taken a job with the Meredith agency as a manuscript reader and was soon promoted to representing a few writers, among them Woolrich. He met that by now wretched and wasted old man, began reading his work, and became both entranced and obsessed. Part of his interest of course was professional--being caught up in Woolrich's world made him a better salesman--but his involvement went way beyond the demands of his job. Just as Scott Fitzgerald and what he stood for had ensnared young Woolrich and dozens of writers of the Woolrich generation, so Malzberg was ensnared by the old Woolrich and the hopelessness with which he saw the world. Perhaps for the first time in his life, that doom-haunted recluse had found a kindred spirit. He felt death coming closer and closer but what he feared even more than death, he told Malzberg that year, was "the endless obliteration, the knowledge that there will never be anything else. That's what I can't stand, to try so hard and to end in nothing." It was as though he believed that if only his writing were good enough he wouldn't have to die. In a powerful chapter included in his book *The Engines of the Night* (1982), Malzberg gives us vivid glimpses of Woolrich's last years, of how he "lived alone ... on the second floor of the Sheraton-Russell Hotel ... surrounded by cases and cases of beer cans and bottles of whiskey and invited the staff to come up and drink beer with him and watch television. Sometimes he would sit in the lobby, more occasionally he would take a cab to McSorley's Tavern" in the Village. His life had crumbled into a pit of alcohol and despair.

His 1967 income totaled less than $8,000 and his record of newly published work added up to two stories, neither within shouting distance of his best. The tale he called "The Synthetic Sleeping-Partner" had been purchased by Dannay for a generous

$425 in the summer of 1966, when adultery was still the only ground for divorce in the state of New York. Dannay ran the story in two installments as "Divorce—New York Style" (*Ellery Queen's Mystery Magazine*, June and July 1967), with a brief premise about the obsolescence of its premise. Steve Dunne, his estranged wife and their lawyers set up the degrading phony-raid-on-love-nest routine which, before the change in the law, was the standard method of establishing adultery in New York courts. But an unseen hand rewrites the script so that, just minutes after the raiding party leaves the hotel room with the photographic evidence, the woman hired to pose for the cameras in bed with Steve is found dead between the sheets. Probably not one of *EQMM*'s hundreds of thousands of readers recognized the situation as a criminous offshoot of Woolrich's 1936 *Breezy Stories* romance "Pick Up the Pieces," or suspected that this "latest" Woolrich whodunit might well have been thirty or more years old. If the tale indeed dates back that far, one can understand why it had taken so long to sell. Woolrich does nothing to develop the premise effectively and makes us settle for a tame, flat story without suspense or detection or interesting characters or emotional fever or *noir* coloration or anything at all to keep us involved. The murder method (nitrobenzene in a bucket of ice cubes) harks back to the Rube Goldberg killing devices in his Thirties pulpers, and the plot details are unforgivably sloppy, with the murderer turning out to have put together all the paraphernalia for the crime at a time when he had no motive and no hope of opportunity! The story has not been included in any subsequent volume of Woolrich's work, and isn't likely to be.

A few months later, in the penultimate issue before his mystery magazine folded, Hans Santesson published a much more rewarding Woolrich tale for which he'd paid a paltry $85. "Intent to Kill" (*The Saint Magazine*, September 1967) is strikingly reminiscent of Woolrich's 1946 classic "The Light in the Window," only this time it's a psychotic veteran of Vietnam—perhaps the first of his kind in crime fiction—who returns to New York and moves through the night streets like a zombie, bent on ritually murdering his wife for one sexual transgression while he was overseas. No one but Woolrich could pack so many wild coincidences into such a tissue-thin storyline, but the *noir* overtones are genuine and the first-person narration believably over-the-edge. At the climax the wife commits suicide under circumstances that convince the husband, first, that he'll be convicted of her murder and, second, that, having *intended* to kill her, he deserves to be convicted. This denouement clearly springs from the distinctive Catholic teaching that one who intends but doesn't actually commit a mortal sin is damned in eternal hell-fire equally with one who goes through with the deed. Where Woolrich picked up this moral tidbit we don't know, whether he believed it himself we don't know, but as a tool to divide our reaction and reflect his protagonist's madness it works like a charm.

During 1967 Woolrich's slow march to the grave quickened

into a fast walk. An ill-fitting shoe led to a bad case of gangrene which "untreated," as Malzberg put it, "turned his leg to charcoal...." His life became even more zombie-like than before. He "would stay in his room and drink almost all the time and stare at the television looking for a film from one of his novels or short stories which came on often enough and usually after 2 A.M.; between the movies and the alcohol he was finally able to find sleep. For a few hours. Until ten or eleven in the morning. When it would all start again."

This was Woolrich's life, if you want to call it living, until April of 1968. "At the end," Malzberg writes, "amidst the cases and the bottles and the empty glasses as the great black leg became turgid and began to stink there was nothing at all. The television did not help, the whiskey left no stain, the bellhops could not bring distraction." As Don Yates recalls what Woolrich later told him, it was "the bellboy who used to bring him his beer" who "realized that something had to be done" and called a doctor. As Mike Avallone remembers it, the credit belongs to Robert L. Fish, who "almost saved Cornell Woolrich's leg from amputation.... But Cornell had procrastinated too long and when Bob saw the pus-stained, bandaged foot ... and alerted the hotel doctor, he was perhaps a day too late. We were all at MWA headquarters waiting for Fish to show up so the board meeting could get underway when Bob burst in, unhappy, delivering the news...." In April he was carried out of the Sheraton-Russell and taken to Wickersham Hospital where his leg was cut off above the knee.

And there in the hospital occurred the last of the many incidents in Woolrich's life whose full dimensions will never be understood. One of the Wickersham chaplains was a priest from the nearby Church of St. John the Baptist. According to Edwin Singer, Woolrich stopped the priest in the hospital corridor one day and said: "Father, I'd like to talk to you. I was born into the [Catholic] faith, and I left the faith, and I'd like to get back in the faith." To which the priest replied: "No problem with that, son. I'll hear your confession, give you absolution, and we'll also give you extreme unction so that you get well." As Singer remembers Woolrich's account of it, he made his confession and received communion either that day or the next. When the attorney asked what had caused this conversion, Woolrich told him that he'd reached the age when he was hearing "Nearer My God to Thee." Singer, a devout Catholic himself, remembers Woolrich afterwards as a placid and subdued man, resigned to the loss of his leg and the coming end of his life.

Woolrich's younger pulp contemporary Steve Fisher was still in Hollywood and had not been in touch for almost twenty years, since the time he'd solicited Woolrich's advice on how to end the *I Wouldn't Be in Your Shoes* movie script. In the month Woolrich lost his leg, Fisher happened to write him "a breezy two-page letter" that somehow got delivered to the hospital. Woolrich wrote a reply "in a large loose scrawl" on the reverse sides of Fisher's pages.

Hello Steve---
It was good to hear from you. You've been in my thoughts so many times over the years. Still young, still dashing, the way we all always stay in our memories of each other. The Steve that wrote *I Wake Up Screaming*....

I came in here at a fast 89 pounds, and with a week left to go. And pulled through minus a gam. I'll be out as soon as my rehabilitation is complete, a little wary and a lot smarter. I'm returning to my father's religion (if they'll have me), the R.C. Not out of fear, but out of gratitude for being given a second time around. Everybody has to have somebody, and I had nobody.

Lots of luck, Steve, and may everything you ever wanted come true.
                              Cornell

What really happened, and why, is anyone's guess. A genuine instance of what Jews call *t'shuvah* and Catholics call conversion? A way of forging a last link with his long-dead father? A reflex of fright? Woolrich can't tell us and the priest won't, and it's none of our business anyway. If his father's nominal faith brought him some peace at the end, few of us would begrudge it to him.

While he was in the hospital, Fred Dannay published the last new Woolrich story to appear in the author's lifetime--and one of the best he'd written in years. "For the Rest of Her Life" (*Ellery Queen's Mystery Magazine*, May 1968) goes back at least to the summer of 1966, when Dannay had paid $350 for it under the title "*Now I've Got You*." It's a grim nightmare of a tale in which a young woman marries a man who turns out to be a sadistic wife-abuser. She meets another man, confesses the truth--which she says makes *her* feel ashamed--and together they try to escape. Every move they make throughout this excruciating story is precisely the wrong thing to do, and Woolrich keeps tightening the screws until we're screaming at them to change their course before it's too late. But each wrong move has also been foreordained in the womb of destiny, and Linda and Garry are the last of the innocent doomed couples whose shattered remains fill the Woolrich world. The story's climax is as dark as anything in the canon, and when it ends, says Harlan Ellison, "you hear your spine crack with tension."

In June he was released from the hospital with an artificial leg on which he could never learn to walk. His last few months were spent back in his room at the Sheraton-Russell, in a wheelchair. In a sense he had become Alan Walker, the protagonist of his own first novel, *Cover Charge*, who also had ended alone and with his legs useless. But at least he had the help of a magnificent hotel staff. "They came to his door with trays, snacks, food, messages, advice," Malzberg writes. "They took good care of him. They helped him down on crutches to

the lobby and put him in the plush chair at the near door so
that he could see the traffic from the street.... They brought
him into the dining room and they brought him out. They took
him upstairs. They took him downstairs. They stayed with him.
They created a subterranean network of concern...."

Thanks to their concern, Woolrich was still alive late in
June when the first major theatrical film based on his work
since *Rear Window* had its New York premiere. *La Mariee Etait
en Noir*, directed by the renowned Francois Truffaut and
adapted from *The Bride Wore Black*, opened on June 25 at the
Festival Theatre, on 57th Street and Fifth Avenue, about a mile
uptown from the Sheraton-Russell. One bright afternoon before
the beginning of the picture's two-and-a-half-month run, Mike
Avallone dropped in at the hotel to fetch Woolrich along to a
private screening. Woolrich balked at going.

"Francois Truffaut will be there!" Avallone told him
excitedly, for the director had made a quick trip to the States
for the premiere. "You know who he is? Just about the
greatest French director working today! He wants to meet the
man whose work he admires so much. Come on, Cornell, I'll
carry you if I have to. Don't you want to see what Truffaut
did with your greatest book?" Avallone kept up the stream of
cajolery and Woolrich in his wheelchair kept staring down at
the floor. Finally, as Avallone remembered when interviewed
for Christian Bauer's documentary, Woolrich spoke. "You're
going to have to leave here, Mickey," he growled, "if you're
gonna keep harping on that. I'm not going. I don't want to
go." It was the only time in his life that Woolrich is known to
have threatened to kick out a visitor; usually, as we've seen, he
got angry when anyone had to leave him. In the end, Avallone
said, "I left him there, still staring at the floor," and went off
to the screening alone.

The movie was still playing at the Festival on July 17
when Don Yates stopped off in New York on the way back to
Michigan after a year in Argentina. Having heard nothing abut
the leg amputation, he gave Woolrich a call as usual. "Oh,
sure," Woolrich said, "come on over, I'll be waiting for you. In
his 1986 interview with Mark Bassett, Yates described what
happened when he reached the Sheraton-Russell.

> I went into the lobby and there he was, in a
> wheelchair, which took me totally by surprise. I said:
> "What happened?"
> He said: "Well, come on upstairs."
> We got on the elevator and went upstairs to his
> room ... on the second floor.
> And he said: "I'm going to show you something....
> I have a prosthetic leg now." He had lost one leg,
> the right leg had been amputated halfway between the
> thigh and the knee. And he said: "I want to show
> you something," and started wiggling out of his pants.
> He said: "I'm not making a pass at you. Understand
> that. I want you to take a look at this."

> And he pulled off the prosthetic leg and threw it across the room, as if he had great scorn for it and hatred, and said: "Look at this." And he showed me the stub of his leg. He said: "Does that look infected to you?"
> I said: "Well, Con, I don't know, I'm not a doctor. It does look raw, it doesn't look very healthy, but I can't tell you if it's infected or not."
> He said: "Well, I just wanted your idea on it. I don't know what I'm going to do about this. I hate this thing."

In his unpublished memoir of Woolrich, Yates described his own reaction and Woolrich's mood in greater detail. "I started to try to play down the seriousness of his disability because that was what he seemed eager to hear. But I was deeply concerned. And he was terrified beyond words of what was going to happen to him. I didn't comprehend it then, only later. Death had moved into that lonely hotel room...." Woolrich's adoption of his father's religion does not seem to have consoled him for long. On the other hand, in my own 1987 interview Yates mentioned that on this visit Woolrich was "more quiet, a little bit more resigned" than usual, so perhaps Edwin Singer's perception of a Woolrich fortified by faith for a peaceful death has some validity too. And yet there was no way, immobilized as he was, that he could get out of his hotel room to attend Mass and receive the sacraments, and he does not seem to have asked any priest to come and visit him. The mystery surrounding the religious aspect of his youth repeats itself in the mystery surrounding the religious aspect of his last months.

Yates was as eager to see Truffaut's movie version of *The Bride Wore Black* as Avallone had been three weeks before, and especially eager to see it with Woolrich beside him.

> I asked Con if he'd seen it. He said: "No, I haven't seen it." I said: "Let's go out and have a look at your movie." Con said: "We'll do that." And I thought it would be great for Woolrich to see a new movie again. What a thrill! And the evening wore on. We didn't have dinner out. He didn't have much of an appetite then. We got to talking, and he was drinking only beer, and I was having some bourbon that he bought for me. And we kept on talking and kept on talking and after a while I knew that we weren't going to go out. And I made one more reference to it, and he said: "Well, let's not bother about that." And I think [that] from the beginning, when I suggested it, he didn't want to say no but he didn't want to go, because he didn't want to leave the hotel in that wheelchair. He didn't want to be seen in a wheelchair.... I didn't press it any further. So I don't believe he ever had the chance to see the film.

Finally in the hours after midnight Yates said goodbye, and this time, he says in his memoir, "there were no recriminations when I said I'd like to leave." Perhaps he had an intuition that he'd never see the man again. Before he left, he asked Woolrich for a manuscript as a sort of souvenir. "So he went to his closet, unlocked it, and brought me the typescript of one of his last stories...." It was the tale which he had called "*Now I've Got You*" and which had appeared in the May *EQMM* as "For the Rest of Her Life."

Yates had brought with him some of his extensive Woolrich collection--hardcover and paperback first editions, old pulp magazines in which the author's stories had been printed long ago--and now asked Woolrich to sign them for him.

> ....I had them in a big shirtbox from the dry cleaner's that I'd wrapped up and brought with me. That was my last request. He said: "Oh, sure, I'd be glad to do that." He said: "You can pick them up tomorrow downstairs." And there was not the bitterness in our farewell that there had been so many nights before, when he seemed terribly angry and disappointed and let down because I was going to leave him alone.
>
> So he said goodbye, and I came back the next morning, and there were the books, waiting for me downstairs. I checked through them and they were all signed, in his very typical and fluid hand. All the Woolrich books were signed as by Woolrich, and all the Irish books were signed as by Irish. It was a last gesture, I guess, of his sense of friendship with me....

In the last weeks of his life Woolrich looked decades older than his actual age, which was sixty-four. He had, wrote Barry Malzberg, "the stunned aspect of the very old. Where there had been the edges there was now only the gelatinous material that when probed would not rebound." But his eyes were still "open and moist, curiously childlike and vulnerable."

On September 19 at 8:35 P.M. Central Daylight Time, Don Yates in East Lansing placed a long-distance call to Woolrich at the Sheraton-Russell to see how he was getting along. In his memoir he describes that call and its aftermath.

> The operator answered, and I said: "May I speak to Cornell Woolrich, please?"
>
> There was a long pause, too long a pause, and that seemed strange to me.
>
> She said: "Are you a friend to Cornell Woolrich?"
>
> And I said: "Yes, I am. Could I speak with him, please?"
>
> She said: "Well," as if searching for words, "something's happened. Mr. Woolrich has been found unconscious, and he's just a minute ago been taken out in an ambulance to the hospital."

I was, of course, dumbstruck by the fact. So I said: "I'll call back tomorrow and see what information you can give me."

I called back the next day and she was able to give me the name of the doctor who was treating him. I called the doctor and he said that [Woolrich] had suffered a stroke and was unconscious.

I said: "Well, I'll call you back again and find out how he's doing."

He said: "That'll be all right."

The days passed, and I called, and he remained in a coma. On the 25th of September—that would be six days after he lost consciousness—he died.

It seems strange to me that the last manifestation of our friendship was my call to him at an instant when he was in great need but it was too late for me to do anything for him. I missed his last words perhaps by a minute or so.

It's a friendship that I'll always prize, because I think he was an enormously gifted writer. And maybe part of his gift was the fact that he was a haunted man as well. I never remember anyone who acted [so much] in his waking hours as if he were living in some kind of dream. It was always lurking in the background, the fringes of his conversation. There was always somehow an expression in his eyes, sometimes painful but never disappearing.

On September 25, 1968, two and a half months short of his sixty-fifth birthday, the dream ended and the specter of Anahuac came for him, the glass was lifted and the fly released from life, into eternal torment or eternal joy, or perhaps, as he believed for all but at most the last few months of his dream, into nothingness.

Further Gems from the Literature
William F. Deeck

And Wolfe has the gall to say "contact" isn't a verb?

"... It is improper for the defense counsel even to talk with me, let alone arrange an interview for me with his client. You, as the wife of a man on trial for his life, are under no such prescription."--"The Next Witness," by Rex Stout

Fleming Stone, master detective, pontificates:

"There's a great deal of human nature in people," he said....--*The Clue of the Eyelash*, by Carolyn Wells

Oxymoron department:

"Now, miss," continued the constable in patient exasperation....--*Death-Watch*, by John Dickson Carr

It's not easy being a Watson, or why are we here:

"I suggest we have a look around," Moreton said impatiently....
Serge regarded him commiseratively. "One can understand your temperamental energy," he said quietly, "but this is mostly a game of patience, Moreton, and a wrong move at this juncture might precipitate disaster...."--*The Merrivale Mystery*, by James Corbett

You can't fool a famous detective:

...He [George Merrivale the invalid] could change his expression without effort, and this signified great mobility of thought and temperament. Serge saw at a glance that he was dealing with an intellectual....--*The Merrivale Mystery*, by James Corbett

William F. Deeck, "Further Gems from the Literature"

Our forgetful authors:

"Who was it, Nick, who coined the phrase, 'The only good Indian is a dead Indian'?"
"Phil Sheridan," he said without a pause.
Not bad. "Exactly," I said.—*The Siskiyou Two-Step*, by Richard Hoyt

Lyle was said to look like the actor Frank B. Ryan, famed for his portrayal of General William Tecumsah Sherman, the man who charmed the world with the sacking of Atlanta and who coined the phrase, "The only good Indian is a dead Indian."—*Cool Runnings*, by Richard Hoyt

New-word department:

"Arouge wasn't exactly sweet. He didn't fragrate."—*Death in Four Colors*, by Brandon Bird

Unfortunate side-effects department:

"You'll have to have a dye injection, which may make you a little nauseous...."—*The Episode*, by Richard Pollak

Department of dubious word selection:

Ever uppermost to nag her was the question of where were Eleanor's personal things, the keepsakes, the little mementos of sentiment which surely must have been indigent to this room?—*Secret Beyond the Door [Museum Piece No. 13]*, by Rufus King

"Until just recently she never had a thought that he might be straying from the strait and narrow."—*Price Tag for Murder*, by Spencer Dean

McNaghten was being pressurised from above.—*The Supreme Adventure of Inspector Lestrade*, by M.J. Trow

"Hester, my dear, you are positively radiant.... As serene and lovely as an angle."—*Skulldoggery*, by Fletcher Flora

"You can accept my assurance that Meredith & Scott will be anxious to facilitate the Yard...."—*Red Dagger*, by James Corbett

He wrote in his little notebook "Curse of the River god" and looked at it approvingly. He knew that there was an enormous credulous section of the public who delighted in occult love and mysterious Eastern curses.—*The Scoop*, by Agatha Christie, et al.

Incidentally it occurred to him that Cora Jackson was an exceedingly attractive girl, with something about her that magnetized him....--*Red Dagger*, by James Corbett

How's-that-again? department:

He came toward her car, with that long free stride and indefinable look of race that had caught her eye among all the other blue uniforms.--*My True Love Lies*, by Lenore Glen Offord

That had been a sound on the other side of the door to Kerr Cameron's office, a sound like something that wasn't there.--*Death in Four Colors*, by Brandon Bird

When his risibilities were agitated he took it out in pulling a pig-tail or throwing a cap or sweater in the branches of a tree.--*Thirteen Men*, by Tiffany Thayer

"I can only say," I replied at length, "that it seems perfectly conceivable that Mrs. Frood could have been at that place, or even near it, unless she went there for some specific purpose--unless, for instance, she were lured there in some way."--*The Mystery of Angelina Frood*, by R. Austin Freeman

She knew she must get rid of this man Savage before her aunt returned, for he was the type who would prey on her mind all night.--*Red Dagger*, by James Corbett

His rather large nose was indicative of talent....--*Death Stops the Rehearsal*, by Richard M. Baker

He still watched every movement, saw Serge's wonderful instruments pass over the body, the magnetic lens and gleaming microscope....--*The Merrivale Mystery*, by James Corbett

"Of course it is possible that one of them has got entangled with the real murderer, but highly improbable. The cook is a respectable widow and the maid has a sweetheart in Devon."--*Jack O'Lantern*, by George Goodchild

She laid a hand on the doorknob and turned it, went inside and stopped, as though galvanised into sudden immobility.--*The Somerville Case*, by James Corbett

"We'll go to the obvious place first," snapped back Phillips. "People with a sense of false security generally go home."--*The Somerville Case*, by James Corbett

Neatest tricks of the week:

His eyes wrinkled and lifted his mustache off his teeth.--*Death in Four Colors*, by Brandon Bird

William F. Deeck, "Further Gems from the Literature"

They were dark eyes, and kindly; they spoke a desire to enter.--*Seven Keys to Baldpate*, by Earl Derr Biggers

"I am of Fairfield, look," the proprietor's eye seemed to be saying.--*The Witch of the Low Tide*, by John Dickson Carr

Felicia's prominent front teeth gave her a contralto voice.--*Death in Four Colors*, by Brandon Bird

Messiest trick of the week:

There was no question that his anguish was sincere. The man had literally gone to pieces before their eyes.--*The White Cottage Mystery*, by Margery Allingham

MYSTERY MOSTS: HERO ROLES

Two actors tie for portrayal of the most different series heroes in talking films. They are David Niven--who played Raffles once in the last film about him (simply entitled *Raffles*, 1940), the borderline mystery hero known as the Scarlet Pimpernel, once in the last film about him (*The Elusive Pimpernel*, 1950), and one of the several James Bonds in *Casino Royale* (1967), which did not signal the end of the Bond films--and Warren William.

William would be the hands-down winner if we counted his Ted Shayne character from the spoofing *Satan Met a Lady*, the "middle version" of the three filmings of *The Maltese Falcon*. Among his more legitimate hero roles, he more often played the hero repeatedly. These began with the first four Perry Mason films: *The Case of the Howling Dog* (1934), *The Case of the Curious Bride* (1935), *The Case of the Lucky Legs* (1935), and *The Case of the Velvet Claws* (1936), it the last of which Mason and Della comprised a husband and wife team. He played Philo Vance just once, but in the most interesting Vance film, *The Gracie Allen Murder Case* (1939). The same year he began appearing in the Lone Wolf movies with *The Lone Wolf Spy Hunt*. He was to appear as Michael Lanyard more times than any other actor, following up with *The Lone Wolf Strikes*, *The Lone Wolfe Meets a Lady*, *The Lone Wolf Keeps a Date* (all 1940), *The Lone Wolfe Takes a Chance*, *Secrets of the Lone Wolf* (both 1941), *Counter-Espionage* (1942), *One Dangerous Night*, and, finally, *Passport to Suez* (both 1943). (Jeff Banks)

Verdicts

Book Reviews

Catherine Aird. *Harm's Way.* Doubleday, 1984; Bantam, 1985.

Detective Inspector C.D. Sloan and Sergeant Crosby are together again in one of Aird's leisurely English mysteries. Horridly, a human finger is dropped by a crow at the feet of a young woman walking one of the public footpaths across a thriving farm. The lengthy hunt for the rest of the body takes both police and footpath group across the fields of four farms. Thus we are introduced to the Mellots, owners of the central farm; to Mrs. Andrina Ritchie, whose husband has just left her; to Sam Bailey and his wife, old-style farmers whose alcoholic son has left home; and to Paul Hucham, bachelor sheep-raiser. George Mellot's brother Tom is owner of a large business recently raided in a takeover attempt by an over-extended financier who has since gone missing. When the body is found, in a highly unusual place, its head is not there, making identification impossible. Another complication is that something strange is going on in Dresham Wood. As Sloan and Crosby learn more about the area and its people, suspicion turns from one possibility to another. The identity of the murdered man is held off for a smashing finish. Good Aird is always a good read, and this is excellent Aird. (Maryell Cleary)

Lilian Jackson Braun. *The Cat Who Played Brahms.* Jove, 1987.

Jim Qwilleran and Siamese cats Koko and Yum Yum are back, after an absence from print of almost twenty years. Qwill is an investigative reporter for the *Daily Fluxion*, relegated in past years to the food and art beats. His investigations have always turned up murders, and his talented cat, Koko, who has a keen nose for clues, is his chief assistant in solving them. Actually, Koko is more the detective, with Qwill his interpreter, often led to the big unabridged dictionary where scratches are more than just scratches. This time around, Qwill is unhappy with the city, so he takes off for a three-month vacation up north, in a lakeside cabin belonging to his eighty-nine-year-old aunt-by-courtesy, Fanny Klingenschoen. The ways of the wilds are mysterious indeed to Qwill. There is a sunken grave outside his window—he thinks. Someone is walking on the cabin roof at night, so he believes. And there definitely are strange going's-on in the old fishing boat and at the turkey farm. The whole town of Mooseville seems to know what's going on, but no one will talk about it. In a short two weeks Qwill makes new friends and learns much about small-town ways. The biggest surprise of all comes when Aunt Fanny dies. Yes, there is a murder or two, but they're almost side issues compared to all the small-town intrigues. (Maryell Cleary)

Lilian Jackson Braun. *The Cat Who Played Post Office.* Jove, 1987.

The surprise at the end of the last book brings Qwill to Pickax City to live in the old Klingenschoen mansion. Accustomed as I was to an always financially embarrassed Qwill, I wasn't sure I could adapt to a wealthy Qwill as the leading citizen of a north-woods town. I needn't have worried. He's still the same Qwill, with the same nose for trouble and the same cats to help him out. The portrayal of an amnesiac Qwill, in the hospital after being run down by a truck, is hilarious. He's become a danger to someone by peering too closely at the disappearance of a housemaid five years before. Now, with some old friends from the city, Iris Cobb and Arch Riker, and new friends from his summer in the cabin (*The Cat Who Played Brahms*), he and Koko solve the mystery. Braun's light touch is delightful; her books are always humorous, with the cats playing major roles. In this one the pleasures of a middle-aged bachelor adjusting to great wealth are particularly likely to evoke chuckles. All cat and Qwill lovers will be glad to know that there are enough loose ends to give us hope for still another book. (Maryell Cleary)

John Sherwood. *The Mantrap Garden.* Scribner's, 1986; Ballantine, 1987.

The famous historic garden at Monk's Mead is no longer lovely; it has suffered neglect and vandalism. Its owners, the Lindsay family, are at odds with one another. Its gardeners are worse than incompetent. Its tutelary dignitary, a statue of poet Anthony Mortlock, Mary Lindsay's brother killed in World War II, has been dressed up in women's underclothing. Dead animals are distributed around the place. Celia Grant, botanist, nursery gardener, and amateur detective, is persuaded to join the Board and find out what is wrong. She learns that Sir Julian Lindsay has been badly beaten up, that Mary Lindsay is suspected of having provided her aged mother with the wherewithal for an easy death, that there is some mystery connected with the dead poet, and then, in the midst of all this, a Frenchman who seems to have no connection with the Lindsays is killed on their doorstep. Grant's intelligence and wit grace the book; she is quickly onto every hint of something strange, talking to people, investigating Anthony's war record, the poems he wrote, and the love affair he wrote about. She rapidly traces the vandalism to a time before Mrs. Mortlock's death, and connects many seemingly disparate events into one coherent account of cover-up, blackmail, and murder. Though gardeners may not be happy with the ending, they will sympathize with the difficulties of keeping up this historic garden. And they, as well as those of us who don't know one plant from another, will find this fast-paced mystery a treat. (Maryell Cleary)

Doris Miles Disney. *Mrs. Meeker's Money.* Doubleday, 1961; Zebra, 1987.

Mrs. Ulysses S. Meeker, widow of a very wealthy man, has spent her widowhood administering his estate. She has given substantially to the library, the park, the hospital, and to the scholarship fund which was her husband's particular interest. At seventy-nine she finally indulges herself: she hires a private detective to locate the grandson of her youthful love. After several months of reports and expense vouchers, she discovers that she is being cheated. Angry, she calls the police chief and then calls upon the postal inspector, intent on catching and prosecuting the thief. Before Inspector Madden can talk further with her, she is killed. Now Madden and his inspector-in-training must track down a murderer. Their step-by-step investigation soon uncovers the culprit, but evidence is lacking. More effort brings solid evidence to light. Nothing exciting about this book, but the details of a postal investigation are interesting. (Maryell Cleary)

Freeman Dana [Phoebe Atwood Taylor]. *Murder at the New York World's Fair.* Countryman Press, 1987, with introduction by Dilys Winn and afterword by Ellen Nehr.

Hang on to your hats and jump into this book ready for a fast-moving tour of the 1939 World's Fair with an energetic sixty-seven-year-old, Daisy (Mrs. Boyleston) Tower. Meet her first in a laundry truck, wearing the cook's clothes, in a getaway from her nephew Egleston's Early American house in suburban Boston, intent on getting to the Fair. Get there she does, on the private train of a nasty millionaire. She is accompanied on her further escapades by Cherry Chipman, her former companion, Sam Minot, a recently fired journalist, a butcher (or is he an art thief?) named Whitty, and a sometime actress who carries a mysterious suitcase with her everywhere. An unidentified corpse appears on the train, and soon Daisy and her friends are attempting to elude the police. They dash around the Fair dressed as guides, changing into other costumes as events permit. Mrs. Tower is mother of a well-known and enterprising newspaperman, now in China, and she matches him for enterprise and sense of humor. Determined not to be shunted back to Boston and the uncaring care of niece-in-law

Elfrida, Daisy decides to solve the mystery on her own. And she does. Don't expect an orthodox mystery with careful plotting and development of characters. Read this book to enjoy the fun. In her introduction, Dilys Winn is less than commendatory, insinuating that, though any Taylor may be better than none, she's not so sure about this one. But, she says, "there is one saving grace. Slapstick." Yes, indeed, slapstick for laughter. Enjoy it for that, and when you've finished, read Ellen Nehr's afterword to learn how it all came to be. (Maryell Cleary)

R.D. Brown. *Hazzard*. Bantam, 1986, 262 pp., $2.95.

Fictional private eyes, especially those in series, typically follow the mold of Philip Marlowe (loner) or Sam Spade (small independent, with secretary and, infrequently, a partner). Big agency private detectives in the Continental Op pattern are rarer, but the rarest of all--probably so different as to ordinarily not really be considerable as private-eye books at all--are those about the heads of large agencies. Alan Nixon had a short-lived series of that sort in the late 1960s or early 1970s, and there are the infrequent books about the Dan Kearney Agency from Joe Gores. And now there are also the Hazzard books by Brown.

The first one, at least, is certainly a private-eye book, with the hero (despite owning a franchise in a large national agency) operating virtually alone, with local and federal law enforcement agencies seemingly as much against him as the major international criminal who is the book's chief villain. In fact, since he is the chief suspect in the murder of his estranged wife, Cheney Hazzard might qualify better as an amateur sleuth or even a suspense hero thrust into an impossible situation not of his own making, but for his background in private investigations.

He is setting up in business in South Texas (good local color) even as he is trying to solve his own wife's murder, protect his stepchildren, and recover a lost million dollars for the gang lord (who is not Mafia nor a Colombian drug smuggler, but rather a current-generation version of Pancho Villa). There are some surprises, and the hero is clever and resourceful.

Given all that, this first book in the series is highly recommended. But this reader wonders if the level can be maintained when the business is established and flourishing, as it seems certain to be doing by the time of the second book. Also, it appears that the hero will then have a wife, and no less a writer than Brett Halliday (the original one, Davis Dresser) tried and pretty largely failed to meld the private-eye and husband-and-wife-team subgenres early in his Mike Shayne series. (Jeff Banks)

Paul Auster. *City of Glass*. Penguin (Contemporary American Fiction), 1987.

I missed this book in its hardcover debut in 1985, and I feel it might have won an Edgar instead of just being nominated if it had received better distribution. This is a fine reading treat for the private-eye fan, of which I rank myself in the forefront. It could not be more highly recommended.

Briefly, private-eye author Dan Quinn (creator of the mildly successful fictional gumshoe Max Work) finds himself working as a private eye when he is hired under the mistaken belief that his name is Paul Auster, "one of the best in the business." His job is to protect a semi-retarded adult son from an abusive father just released from a mental institution. He plunges in and works hard, if not always with the most orthodox methods. But at the end of the book it is unclear whether he has succeeded through no fault of his own (the old man apparently committed suicide) or failed completely (the client and wife have disappeared). Not to worry, the book is the first in a trilogy, all of which will be appearing in Penguin's trade-paperback list, and we can hope such uncertainties will eventually be cleared up.

However, the situation of the hero is more desperate than any previously faced by a private-eye hero at his book's end. He has lost his apartment (due to long absences working on the case), he has lost his identity (getting it confused both with the client *and* with the real Auster, who turns out not to be a private detective either), and he has even surrendered his freedom, becoming a voluntary prisoner in the "isolation room" of his vanished client. Perhaps some of these difficulties will also be ironed out as the series progresses.

A final note: this is one of those gee-I-wish-I-had-had-this-idea books. The knighthood metaphor devised by Chandler for his Marlowe has become one of the "givens" of this subgenre; Auster picks for his hero's model Don Quixote, rather than the ideal figures surrounding Arthur's Round Table, and it is this choice which directs most of the plot turns in a fascinating story. Certainly the book is not a legitimate part of the subgenre, no more than Jules Feiffer's private-detective novel of more than a decade earlier, but it is not one that any devotee of fictional private investigators should miss. (Jeff Banks)

Jonathan Gash. *The Sleepers of Erin.* Dutton, 1983.

Jonathan Gash's hero, Lovejoy, has become well known through a fine BBC-TV series recently aired on cable in the U.S. Lovejoy is perhaps the most endearing rogue hero since Charteris's Saint. Furthermore, many of the (book) series' readers are surely attracted by insights into antiques collecting provided with a lavish hand. And one more plus: Gash is as slick a writer as Bobby Parker.

In this book, Lovejoy becomes embroiled in someone else's scheme to market fake antiques (sleepers) and foils them at the end with his usual mix of brilliance and physical audacity. The book is a stirring read, and Gash's already praised slickness is the major reason. It can mask the fact that the trouble with the law contrived by the villains to force Lovejoy into their hands still remains at the "happy" end of the book. More than that, the slickness (an authorial equivalent of the magician's sleight of hand) may even keep the reader from realizing that Lovejoy never surrenders to the pressures put upon him. Now, no one would prize a hero who allowed himself to be too easily maneuvered by the baddies, but this book would have been twice as convincing had the hero *pretended* to be converted to their cause while secretly resisting. Instead, he tries to foil them at every turn, and the book (but only on thinking over what has been read, never in the hot moments of pleasure it provides) loses most of its credibility thereby. (Jeff Banks)

Jon Land. *Labyrinth.* Gold Medal, 1986, 374 pp., $3.95.

This book takes the prize (if there is one, and if there isn't there certainly should be) for most unlikely hero. Christopher Locke, the unwilling spy, is a failed English prof and novelist. Before that he was a CIA-training dropout. If the reader can suspended disbelief enough to accept the hero, the book is a brilliant one from its menace (a shadowy Committee committed to the destruction of the world's super-powers which forces top CIA and KGB field men to cooperate against it although their superiors are not informed about the effort), through the villains' project of wiping out food crops (to be replaced with their own super-fast-growing supplies), all the way to the resolution in a dogfight between crop-duster airplanes carrying the plague that will denude U.S. agricultural fields and a ragtag squadron of World War II fighter planes.

Land manages to make it all credible, and the ending (when the good guys begin a program of assassinating surviving Committee agents in places of trust around the world) is one that the reader should find most satisfying. Pay your four bucks with a confident expectation of getting your money's worth. (Jeff Banks)

Rex Miller. *Slob.* Signet, 1987, 301 pp.

I got my hands on a "Special Preview Edition Not for Sale" of this paperback original, and so cannot quote the price. However, as I think it unlikely the tab will come to more than five dollars, I can recommend the book without reservation. This is a truly fine example of the Psychological Suspense subgenre.

The title character, a.k.a. Chaingang, is a psychopathic killer with limited precognitive abilities. Plenty of space is devoted to his abused childhood as a shaping factor, and there are many flashbacks to Vietnam, where he mastered military techniques of murder. In the "here and now" portion of the book, he is operating as a sort of modern-day Jack the Ripper in Chicago (though much more blood-thirsty than the original article), and his nemesis is an on-loan policeman who specializes in serial killings.

Gore flows, with more than a dozen of Chaingang's killings described in more graphic detail than one usually finds in a book. The contest between him and hero Jack Eichord reaches a personal level when (1) Windy City police bigwigs maneuver Jack into fronting a transparent claim that a copy-cat killer who has been apprehended is the original "Lonely Hearts Killer" (so-called because he cuts out the hearts of his victims; only the reader knows that Chaingang eats the hearts until almost the very end), and (2) Eichord's romance with the widow of an early victim is publicized.

Chaingang resents losing credit for his murders and decides he can strike at the lying policeman through the widow and her daughter. Meanwhile, by calling up old favors Eichord has learned about the Vietnam background and partially uncovered a Defense Department experimental program using psychos as hunter-killers against the VC. He also learned about a chink in the monster's seemingly impervious armor.

Pace and suspense is marvelously managed. This is the second best book of this sort since Joe R. Lansdale's *Act of Love*, almost a decade ago. In fact, it is the only book in the subgenre, excepting *Red Dragon*, that I rate better than *Act of Love*. (Jeff Banks)

Steven Olderr. *Mystery Index: Subjects, Settings, and Sleuths of 10,000 Titles.* American Library Association, 1987, 492 pages, $29.95.

Steven Olderr, Director of the Riverside (Ill.) Public Library, the regional resource library of the Suburban Library System, says that this compilation is "an attempt to provide for those patrons access not only to our own collection but to the major body of mystery and detective fiction." If just half of these ten thousand books are available in the Riverside library, I envy those who can borrow books from that system.

In the Main Entry section are listed authors and titles. The author-and-title choices are perforce selective. I checked a few authors that I have written or am writing articles about, and I found no books under Louisa Revell, one book under Percival Wilde, three under Kenneth Hopkins, no books under Kyril Bonfiglioli, and no books under A.E. Martin. Some of your favorites may also be missing, but there ought to be a lot of discoveries of authors unfamiliar to you.

Besides the author-and-title index, there is a separate title index, a 157-page index of subjects and settings, and a 29-page character index that has detectives appearing in the titles listed plus some miscellaneous characters, such as Gracie Allen in S.S. Van Dine's *The Grace Allen Murder Case*, although I would have thought that Gracie Allen was hardly important enough to make the list.

For those who have or have access to the essential crime-fiction reference works, the primary appeal of *Mystery Index* will be the subject-and-setting index. Some of the listings under the category DETECTIVES, for example, are accountants, actors, agoraphobics, air pilots, alcoholic, antiquarians, art dealers, automobile racing drivers, black, blind, book collectors, botanists, deaf, dentists, ecologists, editors, fortune tellers, governesses, gypsy, ichthyologists, and insects, just to select briefly from the early part of the alphabet.

While the subject index is flawed—any index that I have not compiled is flawed, in my opinion, but I must admit I have many biases and a few prejudices about taxonomy in the mystery that would leave others aghast—it is very informative in many areas for those looking for mystery novels dealing, at least to some extent, with specific subjects.

When, for example, I looked under "Elevator," right where it should be was John Rhode's *Fatal Descent.* Splendid. Unfortunately, Craig Rice, rather than Carter Dickson, is given as the co-author. However, in the Main Entry section, Dickson is correctly cataloged.

One category is Mariticide, a wife killing her husband, the reverse of uxoricide, also listed. Mariticide is a word I had never seen or heard. The Oxford English Dictionary, bless it, the only dictionary in which I found the word, says it (the word, not the deed) is rare. I owe Mr. Olderr one for bringing this to my attention.

Under Castration is Joyce Porter's *Dover and the Unkindest Cut of All.* Terrific. Where else would you find such helpful, albeit chilling, information?

On the other hand, *P. Moran, Operative*, by Percival Wilde, is listed under Connecticut, which is a broad reference. It may also be elsewhere, but it is not where it should be, under correspondence-school detectives, and actually there is no such category.

William P. McGivern's *But Death Runs Faster* is listed under Editors, whereas it should be under Editors as Detectives.

Under Father and Daughter Detectives, H.C. Bailey is said to have four titles. Which ones? There's no way of telling. It certainly wasn't any of the Fortunes. While I am not that widely read in the Clunk novels, I don't recall that he had a daughter, and definitely not one who assisted his investigations. I suspect Hilea, rather than H..C., Bailey was meant.

Following Accountants as Detectives is Emma Lathen's *Accounting for Murder*. Accounting, yes, but John Putnam Thatcher, the detective, was not an accountant but a generalist.

There is a category Carters and Catering, which does not mean people who haul food hither and yon; it is actually a typo. It should be Caterers and Catering.

The subject-and-settings section of *Mystery Index*, despite its flaws, is nonetheless helpful. And if in browsing through it you note something in error, do let Mr. Olderr know. The index is obviously a labor of love, and perhaps there will be a second, more correct edition if we all pitch in with suggested corrections.

Recommendation: Prevail upon your library to get Allen J.

Hubin's *Crime Fiction, 1749-1980: A Comprehensive Bibliography* (Garland Publishing) and the supplement for 1981-85 coming out early this year from Garland.

Equally essential but in another category is Walter Albert's *Detective and Mystery Fiction: An International Bibliography of Secondary Sources* (Brownstone Books, whoever they may be). This should be your library's second acquisition. And if the library won't get Albert's book, shame on them.

If it is impossible to persuade your library to spend the sums necessary for those two reference works, then the library should be willing to get *Mystery Index*. After all, it's published by the ALA and the price is reasonable, comparatively speaking. It is no substitute for Albert's bibliography and it's an inadequate substitute for Hubin, but it's a hell of a lot better than nothing.

Should you have convinced your library to get all three books, my congratulations. Now slowly but sneakily push for Albert J. Menendez's *The Subject Is Murder, Twentieth Century Crime and Mystery Writers* (don't ask me which edition; shoot for both), Pronzini and Muller's *1001 Midnights*, Barzun and Taylor's *A Catalogue of Crime*, and Bourgeau's *The Mystery Lovers Companion*. Or buy them yourself if you have lost all control, as I have, and must have these books by your bedside. I'll be buying *Mystery Index* and making notes. (William F. Deeck)

Spencer Dean. *Price Tag for Murder*. Doubleday, 1959; Pocket Books, 1961, 184 pages.

This is one more in the series of interminable—if this novel is any guide—adventures of Don Cadee, Chief of Store Protection at Ambletts Fifth Avenue. As information comes to Cadee's attention that an entire warehouse of merchandise, a warehouse that should have had no existence, has disappeared, he is simultaneously faced with the suicide or murder of a key employee in the store's purchasing department. Some minor problems for Cadee are the installation of a closed-circuit television to scan areas in the store and the perhaps imminent departure of a company executive to Mexico, possibly accompanied by some of the store's funds and one of the store's best buyers.

For those who like action, or what seems like it, and dialogue, with very little description or writing style and not a whole lot of plot. (William F. Deeck)

John Rhode. *Dead of the Night*. Dodd, Mead, 1942; Collins, 1942, as *Night Exercise*; Popular Library, no date, 221 pages.

This is the first novel by Rhode that I have read, aside from his collaboration with Carter Dickson, that does not feature Dr. Priestly. Though I find Priestly's cases generally interesting, Priestly himself I regard as more than a bit of a bore. The characters in this novel appeal, however.

Dead of the Night has something of the flavor of Christiana Brand's *Green for Danger*. Though it's not as good as her book, how many novels are? Whereas hers was about the activities in a hospital undergoing air raids during World War II, this deals with training and preparations for the potential invasion of England by Germany.

The Home Guard of Wealdhurst is taking part in a night drill along with the Civil Defense Services. Colonel Chalgrove, the Group Commander and a man heartily detested by most who know him, shows up unexpectedly to observe the drill. The Colonel then vanishes during the exercise.

Many explanations are given for the Colonel's disappearing act. All of them turn out to be unsatisfactory.

Suspicion begins to point to Major Ledbury, commander of Wealdhurst's Home Guard, as the man who murdered Chalgrove, though there is no body. There is also, to my mind, little reason to suspect him, other than a mild threat to do grievous bodily harm to the Colonel because of the Colonel's officiousness, a threat also uttered or thought by others. The detective, an otherwise estimable chap, blunders badly here, and Ledbury has to find out what happened to save himself.

Rhode provides what seems to be a realistic picture of wartime England as well as a better-than-average mystery. (William F. Deeck)

Austin J. Small. *The Master Mystery.* Doubleday Crime Club, 1928, 341 pages.

Everything red in Gairlie Castle disappears sooner or later, usually sooner. On the night that the betrothal of Lord Gairlie's daughter, Lonora, to Tommy Delayn, all-round sportsman, dilettante chemist, and recent pauper, the Gairlie Rubies, 811 perfect stones, are stolen. Since Delayn was left alone to watch the room containing the rubies, he is naturally accused, as the room was—and here we have to take the word of the author—hermetically sealed except for the door at which he was standing lookout.

While Delayn is in jail, a housemaid is murdered in the library. There are no marks on her body, but her purple uniform is stained an uneven red, with streaks of vivid scarlet, and there are pieces of glass in her clothing. Then a Scotland Yard detective is found dead, under the same circumstances in the same room—a windowless room with only one door, and that door being watched in his case.

Another detective, in the hope of capturing whatever it is committing the murders, stakes out the library, with the room being observed closely by his colleagues. He fires his gun, and when the others rush into the room they find it unoccupied except for his corpse. His clothes, too, have red streaks. Meanwhile, the removal of all red items continues.

The case is solved—or, more accurately, the criminal, who

could only have been one person, is revealed--by a mysterious and utterly strange person named John Argle, who was in love with the murdered housemaid. Argle spends a fair amount of time impersonating, literally, a statue of Rodin's The Thinker, but he spots the killer while he (Argle), again literally, is up a tree.

Of course, Delayn gets the girl and saves her father from ruination. The locked-room murders are explained to the satisfaction of The Chief, a Scotland Yard man who has no name, but not to this reader. There's at least one gaping hole in the explanation. This novel was no doubt exciting in 1928, but those interested in it today are probably limited to impossible-crime fanciers who don't mind straining their credulity. (William F. Deeck)

Frank Shay. *The Charming Murder.* Macaulay, 1930, 255 pages.

This is Frank Shay's first attempt, and that is indeed the operative word, at a mystery novel. There is a fine plot here, one worthy of Queen, Carr, or Christie. As it is worked out, however, it is unworthy of almost anyone.

Dr. Jack Charming is an unhappy man, for several undeniable reasons: He is a millionaire and he is irresistible to women. Both of these drawbacks are getting in the way of his practice of medicine, his simple rounds in the hospital, and his marrying the not-yet-divorced fourth wife of a bounder. She appears to be no great catch, but such apparently is love.

Charming has invited seven friends--and with friends like his he has no need for enemies--for cocktails and a buffet. At about 9:45 p.m. off they all go to the theater, followed by drinks at a nightclub, and then back to the doctor's apartment. The doctor sends in his guests and keeps the taxi to take home the woman he wants to marry. The guests go into the apartment to discover the police, who inform them that Dr. Charming was shot dead in the apartment while they--well, most of them; things are a bit unclear here--were all there about 9:30 p.m.

A nifty puzzle to work out, eh? Does the author accomplish the feat? Yes. Is it satisfactory? No.

The first-person narrator, a newspaperman of the not-too-bright breed that was prominent in those days, tells the reader in a prologue that "no one, save these same guests and his servants," had access to Dr. Charming's apartment at the time of the murder. He lies. At least five others did, and there was only one servant.

The stage presentation that the group goes to see is Professor Proteus, an impersonator. During his act, he impersonates George Washington delivering his "Farewell Address to his Generals"--no, I hadn't known about this, either. His impersonation is "pure genius," although how anyone would be able to judge is beyond me.

Getting closer to the present, Proteus makes himself up like Abraham Lincoln and delivers the Gettysburg Address. The audience stamps on the floor after this performance, presumably in approval. Perhaps some of them were there for the original and remember it well.

Finally, in the here and now, Proteus makes himself up to look like Charles Lindbergh standing in front of the "Spirit of St. Louis." No remarks this time--what would they be?--but the house shakes with applause. A little authorial license here, one presumes. Proteus is obviously on to a good thing with this group.

Then, as a departure from his regular act, Proteus says he will make himself up to look like a member of the audience. Dr. Charming is chosen, and Proteus does such a good job that even Charming's friends can't tell him from the good doctor.

It turns out that Proteus has been paid by one of the Doctor's party to impersonate him. Why? I don't know, Proteus doesn't know, and if the author knows, he isn't splitting.

A police sergeant, the newspaper reporter, and the widower of the woman Dr. Charming wanted to marry--yes, she's dead, too, murdered about the same time as the Doctor but in a different place--are returning from the dead woman's apartment. The widower won't answer the sergeant's questions, so the sergeant turns a flashlight on him and discovers that the man's pupils do not respond to light, which means he's either dead or the sergeant thinks he is. The sergeant gets out of the taxi and tells the driver to take the corpse to the morgue. Ah, those were simpler days!

The doctor's apartment, joined to his office, is on the ground floor. In one of the many summings-up by police lieutenant Daniel (Deedee) Doner, he has one of the suspects going upstairs. One of the suspects is shot and killed while in the apartment, apparently by someone who thought he and the victim were on the second floor.

Four people enter the apartment through a door that only the police have noticed. The reason it has not been noticed is that it is blocked by a steel cabinet. The question of how that group got through the steel cabinet is never raised.

The group of four contained a gangster, his hit man who was supposed to kill Charming, and two people who were to play other roles but would have made excellent witnesses to the murder, something that seems not to have occurred to the gangster. Something else had not occurred to the gangster, and who this time can blame him? "I hears someone in the bathroom and when I whispers to 'em to lay quiet the guy with the gun lets it go off." Good hit men have always been hard to find. Luckily for the gangster, someone else had already shot Charming.

The man impersonating Charming--not Professor Proteus, remember--was dubious about being able to do the job successfully, but after "trailing" Charming for several days he is able to fool Charming's friends, Charming's mistress, and Charming's would-like-to-be mistresses under the most testing of circumstances.

The narrator becomes drunk and starts slurring his words, except when the author forgets to have him do it.

Those who enjoy what Bill Pronzini deems "alternative

classics" ought to appreciate this novel. Others should shun it. (William F. Deeck)

Wirt Van Arsdale. *The Professor Knits a Shroud.* Doubleday Crime Club, 1951, 217 pages.

Pedro Jose Maria Guadaloupe O'Reilly y Apodaca, B.S., M.A., Ph.D., more familiarly and shortly known as Peter or Uncle Pete, is a professor of anthropology, not, as Doubleday's dustjacket would have it, archaeology. The young lady to whom he is a former guardian invites him, somewhat to the displeasure of her husband even though he usually enjoys Uncle Pete's company, to their farm, presently occupied by Henri von Fliegel, a best-selling author.

Apodaca describes Von Fliegel's books this way: "Oh, he had good story ideas. That I will grant you. But then he'd take those good ideas and embellish them with all sorts of impossible characters and impossible situations and throw in a lot of cheap sentimentality and as much fornication as he thought he could get by with and call the whole nauseating mess a novel."

Ah, how the literary world has progressed since the 1950s. But I digress.

As is usual with successful authors--though only in fiction, one hopes--Von Fliegel is loathed by almost everyone, and apparently with good reason. As is to be expected, he comes to no good end, shot in the head while working on his current novel.

Luckily, Professor Apodaca's experience in anthropological field work leads him to make some sterling deductions, and these convince the police that he should be part of the investigation. He solves the case, to the appreciation of almost all concerned.

As an aid to his cerebration, the professor knits socks. At last count, he had completed 2,736--individual ones, I believe, not pairs. The only unbelievable item in the novel, if one accepts the sock count, is Apodaca's inability to recall for a lengthy period where he had read about the word *rache* written in blood. There are well-read people who wouldn't immediately know that, but what are they doing detecting in mystery novels?

Wirt Van Arsdale, a pseudonym of Martha Wirt Davis, wrote only one mystery. A pity, for Van Arsdale showed lots of promise in this book. Of course, you have to accept the usual caveat that people act unreasonably for purposes of the plot in this biblio mystery. (William F. Deeck)

Edgar Wallace. *The Green Archer.* Hodder, 1923; Small, 1924; W.W. Norton, 1965, "revised edition" for The Seagull Library of Mystery and Suspense, 192 pages.)

Briefly, which is the kindest way to treat this work, *The Daily Globe* receives word that the Green Archer of Garre

Castle, hanged in 1487, is back again haunting the castle. The castle's owner, Abe Bellamy, late of Chicago and one of the world's worst (in more senses than one) villains, wants no investigation of the haunt's return. Bellamy, the author says, never has spent a night away from the castle since he bought it. This is contradicted in the first part of the book, but never mind.

The first victim of the Archer, killed by an arrow somewhere in his waistcoat, is a man who had recently had a quarrel with Bellamy. The body is found by Spike Holland, an American reporter who is working for *The Daily Globe*. "Spike knelt down at the dead man's side and sought for some sign of life...." Sure. Spike turns over to the police a second green arrow that he finds at the scene of the crime, although the author doesn't tell us how or where he found it. But don't worry; it has nothing to do with anything.

James Lamotte Featherstone is the Scotland Yard man—a captain, if the Yard has such things—who investigates Bellamy. He becomes involved after he is hired by a millionaire to keep an eye on his daughter. If that strikes you as odd, you're definitely not going to enjoy this book, because it is replete with such oddities.

Bellamy gets his just desserts, but not because of Featherstone, who, you will not be surprised to hear, gets the girl whose body he was guarding. Featherstone is vigorous but lackwitted. The same can be said for the heroine. They deserve each other.

The purpose of the Seagull Library of Mystery and Suspense was to "restore to print hard-cover editions of famous favorites and classics regarded by connoisseurs as indispensable collectors' items." P.G. Wodehouse once said that nine hundred of every thousand books by Wallace were worth the money. Why did the publishers have to select one of the other hundred to reprint? (William F. Deeck)

The Documents in the Case

(Letters)

From Jeff Banks, P.O. Box 13007, SFA Station, Nacogdoches, TX 75962:

I am elated by the two results of the poll. Continuation is a treat, and I am also pleased that you are finally taking my advice about discontinuing payment.

In the current issue [9:4], I suppose I liked the Hazeltine article best. Thinking back over the marvelous history of your publication, my favorite subjects for articles are (1) Spillane, (2) pulps, (3) radio, and not just because I have written most of my contributions on those subjects. Among the reviews, my favorites are those of private eye books, because that is my favorite type of book to read.

Marvin Lachman is certainly your most faithful columnist and always a treat to read. And of the article series, Deeck's "Gems" is my favorite—and not just because he seems to pick more often on the private dicks than other subgenresh!

My commentary is briefer this time as we are in the end-of-school rush, now peaking with final exams. And based on your plea for book reviews, I felt perhaps you would rather I spend timie on them than a letter.

Happy 20th Birthday, TAD!

Celebrate TAD's first two decades with this money-saving combination: a hardcover facsimile reprint of TAD's first volume and a trade paperback collection of eighteen essays and reminiscences on TAD's early days by founder Al Hubin and more than a dozen other luminaries who made it all happen. Both books—a $29.95 value—are available direct from Brownstone Books for $25.00 postpaid. Save $4.95 and treat yourself to hours of pleasurable reading in the company of TAD's leading lights:

> *The Armchair Detective*, Volume One, smythe-sewn and bound in quality cloth, this facsimile reprint contains all 158 pages of the first four issues of TAD, plus a specially written introduction by Allen J. Hubin; viii, 158 pp., available individually for $17.00 postpaid.

> *TAD-SCHRIFT: Twenty Years of Mystery Fandom in The Armchair Detective*, edited by J. Randolph Cox, this quality trade paperback contains essays by Bob Adey, Jon L. Breen, Robert E. Briney, Joe R. Christopher, J. Randolph Cox, William K. Everson, John A. Hogan, Estelle Fox, Marvin Lachman, Edward S. Lauterbach, Frank D. McSherry, Jr., Francis M. Nevins, Jr., William F. Nolan, John Bennett Shaw, Charles Shibuk, Donald A. Yates, and a long survey of TAD's first decade by founder and long-time editor Allen J. Hubin; vii, 111 pp., available individually for $12.95 postpaid.

Also Available from Brownstone Books

Detective and Mystery Fiction: An International Bibliography of Secondary Sources, edited by Walter Albert, smythe-sewn and bound in quality cloth, this Edgar winner belongs on the reference shelf of every mystery fan worthy of the name; xii, 781 pp., $60.00 postpaid.

The Sound of Detection: Ellery Queen's Adventures in Radio, edited by Francis M. Nevins, Jr., and Ray Stanich, this illustrated, quality trade paperback, which consists of a detailed narrative history (by Nevins) of the long-running Ellery Queen radio program and an annotated log (by Stanich and Nevins) of the individual episodes, is a must for Queen fans as well as fans of Old Time Radio; viii, 109 pp., $6.95 postpaid.

The Mystery Fancier, second oldest generalist mystery fan publication in the United States (only TAD has been around longer), is now published quarterly in a trade-paperback format. A year's subscription is $25.00 (second class), $30.00 (first class in U.S. and Canada), or $35.00 (airmail overseas). Individual issues are $7.50 postpaid.

In the Brownstone Chapbook Series

Volume One: *Hardboiled Burlesque: Raymond Chandler's Comic Style*, by Keith Newlin, 50 pp., $4.95 postpaid.

Volume Two: *The New Hard-Boiled Dicks: A Personal Checklist*, by Robert E. Skinner, vii, 60 pp., $6.95 postpaid.

Volume Three: *John Nieminski: Somewhere a Roscoe*, selected and edited by Ely Liebow and Art Scott, 61 pp., $6.95 postpaid.

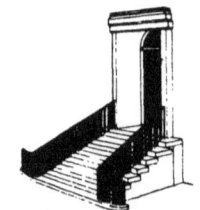

Brownstone Books
407 Jefferson Street
Madison, Indiana 47250
(812/265-2636)

www.ingramcontent.com/pod-product-compliance
Lightning Source LLC
Chambersburg PA
CBHW031435040426
42444CB00006B/826